With Hitler to the End

Heinz Linge with Hitler and Martin Bormann, Salzburg, June 1943

With Hitler to the End

The Memoirs of Adolf Hitler's Valet

Heinz Linge

Introduction by Roger Moorhouse
Translation by Geoffrey Brooks

Frontline Books, London / Skyhorse Publishing, New York

With Hitler to the End: The Memoirs of Adolf Hitler's Valet

This edition published in 2009 by Frontline Books, an imprint of Pen & Sword Books Limited,
47 Church Street, Barnsley, S. Yorkshire, S70 2AS
www.frontline-books.com

and

Published and distributed in the United States of America and Canada
by Skyhorse Publishing, 307 West 36th Street, 11th Floor, New York, NY 10018
www.skyhorsepublishing.com
Skyhorse Publishing books may be purchased in bulk at special discounts for sales promotion, corporate
gifts, fund raising, or educational purposes. Special editions can also be created to specifications.
For details, contact Special Sales Department, Skyhorse Publishing, 307 West 36th Street, 11th Floor,
New York, NY 10018 or email info@skyhorsepublishing.com.

© 1980 by F.A. Herbig Verlagsbuchhandlung GmbH
Translation © Pen & Sword Books Ltd, 2009
United Kingdom edition © Pen & Sword Books Ltd, 2009
North America edition © Skyhorse Publishing, 2009

Frontline edition: ISBN 978-1-84832-544-9
Skyhorse edition: ISBN 978-1-62636-326-7

Publishing History
Bis zum Untergang: Als Chef des Persönlichen Dienstes bei Hitler (edited by Werner Maser) was first
published in German by Nation Europa Verlag GmbH in June 1980. This is the first English-language
edition of the text and includes a new introduction by Roger Moorhouse.

10 9 8 7 6 5 4 3

A CIP data record for this title is available from the British Library and the Library of Congress.

Library of Congress Cataloging-in-Publication Data

Linge, Heinz, 1913-1980.
 [Bis zum Untergang. English]
 With Hitler to the end : the memoir of Hitler's valet / Heinz Linge ; introduction by Roger Moorhouse.
 p. cm.
 Translation of: Biz zum Untergang. München : Herbig, 1980.
 Includes bibliographical references.
 ISBN 978-1-60239-804-7 (hardcover : alk. paper)
 1. Linge, Heinz, 1913–1980. 2. Hitler, Adolf, 1889–1945. 3. Hitler, Adolf, 1889–1945—Friends and
associates. 4. Germany—Politics and government—1933–1945. 5. Valets—Germany—Biography.
6. Nazis—Biography. I. Title.
 DD247.H5L4813 2009
 943.086092—dc22
 [B]
                                     2009015869

For more information on our books, please visit www.frontline-books.com,
email info@frontline-books.com or write to us at the above address.

Typeset by Wordsense Ltd, Edinburgh

Printed in China

Contents

Illustrations

Introduction

THOUGH THEY MIGHT NOT have known the name, those with an interest in the Nazi period would probably recognise Heinz Linge. In countless photographs of the Führer of the Third Reich, he can be seen in the background, often just behind Hitler. A tall man in SS uniform, with a prematurely receding hairline and a rather lugubrious expression, Linge was Hitler's valet; perhaps the most intimate of his personal staff.

Born in Bremen in 1913, Heinz Linge was a former bricklayer who joined the elite *SS-Leibstandarte*, Hitler's SS bodyguard, in 1933. Two years after that, he was selected to serve on Hitler's household staff, and was appointed as the Führer's personal valet shortly after the outbreak of war in 1939.

In this capacity, Linge was responsible for all aspects of Hitler's household; from day-to-day operations, such as the Führer's wardrobe and diet, to more prosaic duties such as keeping Hitler supplied with reading glasses, pencils and even money. It was Linge who woke Hitler in the morning and assisted him as he retired to bed in the early hours. It was Linge who would man the door to Hitler's office or apartment and who would be pumped by visitors for information on the Führer's mood. It was Linge, indeed, who helped carry Hitler's corpse up to the Reich Chancellery garden on

30 April 1945 and who supervised its hasty cremation. Whether in Berlin, on 'the Berg' at Berchtesgaden or in the Wolfsschanze HQ at Rastenburg, Linge was rarely more than a click of the fingers or a whispered instruction away from his master. He was Hitler's constant companion throughout the war. And, as he himself acknowledged, only Eva Braun stood closer to Hitler than he did.

This position at the very heart of the Third Reich – what he himself called a 'theatre-box on history' – gave Linge a fascinating perspective on the regime and the man that he served. At the centre of his account, of course, is Adolf Hitler himself. Linge's loyalty to Hitler was absolutely unquestioning and unswerving; an attitude that he characterised as one of 'total uncritical obedience'. This was not ideologically motivated, however. Despite his membership of the SS, Linge was no ideologue and paid little heed to political matters. Rather, his loyalty to 'the Boss' was based on much more mundane ideas: on the one hand, it was wholly in tune with that fidelity demonstrated, since time immemorial, by a servant to his master. On the other – as this memoir makes clear – Linge simply considered Hitler to be a genius; one of history's 'great men'.

Despite this, Linge's profile of Hitler does not come across as starry-eyed. His portrayal is affectionate, certainly, but it is not without criticism and it does lack some of the more superficial 'pleasantness' recorded, for instance, by Hitler's secretaries, Traudl Junge and Christa Schroeder.[1] Linge clearly felt a respect for his employer, which it seems was reciprocated. Yet, through a series of anecdotes and observations, he gives tremendous depth and substance to Hitler's character; recounting the daily routine in his household; his eating habits, his foibles, his preferences, his sense of humour and even his obsession with time.

---

1 See Traudl Junge, *Until the Final Hour*, London 2002, and Christa Schroeder, *He Was My Chief: The Memoirs of Hitler's Secretary*, London 2009. Linge was Junge's best man at her wedding in June 1943.

Linge also charts the changes in Hitler's character during the period of his service; for instance when the Führer seemed to have 'lost' his levity of mood – and with it the ability to laugh – in 1940. More seriously, Linge describes Hitler's fading health from around 1942, from which time the role of 'physician to the Führer' became a position to almost rival his own. Most interestingly in this respect, Linge claims to have been present late in 1944, when Hitler suffered some sort of circulatory collapse, and evidently came close to death. He also comments on Hitler's private life, not only refuting the persistent rumours of Hitler's monorchidism but also going further to assert that his employer maintained a normal sex life with Eva Braun.

Linge is certainly unsparing in charting Hitler's physical decline, but he also shows that it is unwise to be too dogmatic about the Führer's supposedly deteriorating mood over the same period. This point is ably illustrated by an anecdote from late in 1944, when Hitler was accidently put through on the telephone to another caller from the SS entourage, who evidently assumed that Hitler's standard greeting of 'This is the Führer' was a joke, and started laughing. Hitler's surprisingly measured and humorous reaction to the incident rather belies the image of him as a rabid and ill-tempered 'carpet-biter'. Indeed, the Hitler that emerges from Linge's memoir is an interesting and multi-faceted individual: unpredictable and demanding, of course, but not of an otherwise unpleasant nature.

This apparently sympathetic portrayal of the Nazi leader might sit uncomfortably with some readers. Yet, we are kidding ourselves if we imagine that Hitler was some one-dimensional monster – all rolling eyes and rabid ranting. He was not. As this book demonstrates, the Hitler that we know – the man who had millions murdered and started the most costly and destructive war in history – also had a human side: he could be affable to his staff, kiss his secretaries' hands and be kind to his dog. If this apparent humanity offends our preconceptions, then perhaps our preconceptions need altering.

Whether we like it or not, Linge's Hitler comes across as a rounded human being, and he is arguably all the more terrifying for that.

Linge does not confine his observations to Hitler, however. Though he was, by his own admission, politically disengaged and even a little naïve, he nonetheless gives engaging accounts of many of the salient events of the period. Of these, the headline story in this book is undoubtedly his assertion that Hitler had had advanced knowledge of Rudolf Hess's flight to Britain in May 1941. Though the official account of that episode held that Hess had flown of his own accord and without Hitler's knowledge – a story that was scrupulously maintained by the regime and has held sway ever since – Linge's instincts and observations told him otherwise.

Few of the members of Hitler's 'court', meanwhile, seem to have impressed Linge. Ribbentrop, he wrote, was 'arrogant', Himmler was 'unimpressive' and 'a pedant', whilst Hess was at least amiable, if utterly unpredictable. He reserved most of his vitriol for Martin Bormann, however, who emerges as a devious, Machiavellian schemer of the first order. Of all the Nazi inner circle, indeed, Linge had the most praise for Josef Goebbels, Hitler's propaganda minister, whom he described as 'genial' and 'amusing', citing Hitler's characterisation of him as 'a giant in a dwarf's body'.

Inevitably, perhaps, Linge would pay dearly for his proximity to Hitler. He had previously imagined that he might be rewarded for his service with a sinecurial position and a country estate, much like the loyal servants of the past who often benefited handsomely from their masters' largesse. However, it was not to be. As manservant to the most infamous dictator of the twentieth century, Linge could scarcely have expected to slink away to a comfortable retirement. After escaping from the Führerbunker in Berlin, on 2 May 1945, he was captured by the Soviets, who – on learning of his former position

– swiftly shipped him to Moscow, to the notorious Lubyanka prison and to the tender mercies of Stalin's NKVD secret police. There, he was subjected to repeated interrogation and frequent torture, with his inquisitors demanding – over and over again – to know every detail of Hitler's life, and painstakingly piecing together the precise circumstances of his death. Finally, Linge was tried and sentenced to twenty-five years imprisonment, of which he served barely five years before being released in the general amnesty of 1955.

Given such tribulations, it should come as no surprise that Linge's memory was not perfect. Though he had a rank in the SS, for instance, he claimed not to have been a Nazi Party member. We now know, however, that he was; having joined the Party in 1932 with the membership number 1,260,490.[2] Nonetheless, it should be noted that Linge has subsequently been proven to be someone whose recollection of events can largely be trusted. After his interrogation in Moscow, for example, a report was compiled for Stalin's attention, which detailed the information gleaned about Hitler from the NKVD's investigations. In that report, Linge (and fellow prisoner, Hitler's former SS-adjutant Otto Günsche) quoted Hitler's speeches and writings from memory, as they had no recourse to published sources during their imprisonment. Yet, as was later established, the recall of both men was found to be very precise, with no notable divergences from the published versions.[3]

Importantly, Linge does not come across as an unreconstructed and unrepentant Nazi. Like many others, he claims ignorance of the most egregious crimes of his masters and his intention in writing this memoir – aside, one imagines, from the obvious financial attraction – appears primarily to have been to refute some of the more fanciful claims that had been made in the post-war period by those claiming to have been close to Hitler. Moreover, he was evidently frustrated

2 Ernst Klee, *Das Kulturlexicon zum Dritten Reich. Wer War Was Vor und Nach 1945*, Frankfurt am Main 2007, p.369.

3 Henrik Eberle and Matthias Uhl (eds), *The Hitler Book*, London 2005, p.xxviii.

by the tendency amongst memoirists to lay every failure and every shortcoming at Hitler's door. 'Scarcely a general can be found', he wrote, 'who admits that he lost a battle by his own bad leadership.' Linge's loyalty to his Führer, it seems, persisted even long after the latter's death.

Whatever his motivation in writing, Heinz Linge is a very engaging chronicler, giving the reader a truly fascinating and enlightening insight into the person of Adolf Hitler, and life at the very heart of the Third Reich. *With Hitler to the End* is a book that – almost thirty years after its first publication and after its author's death – fully deserves to be read and its appearance in this first English-language edition is to be heartily welcomed.

Roger Moorhouse, 2009

Preface

IN 1955 WHEN I returned from ten years' captivity in Russia I was besieged by journalists and publishers wanting my experience of Hitler and his fall. The text of every enquiry, offer and telegram read: 'Please do not sign any contract. We shall offer more.' I decided to accept the offer of an Englishman who had expressly agreed in writing to publish only what I had approved previously. He kept to the bargain, as did other foreign publishers and journalists. Only a German publisher thought my memoir should be 'rephrased' and the content changed. What I finished up reading was nicely put but unrelated to the facts. Inexperienced and powerless against such intrigues, I rejected my attorney's advice to seek legal redress.

A story that irresponsible journalists had cooked up did the rounds as 'The Linge Report' and caused me great harm. Former colleagues from Hitler's entourage turned their backs on me, and the intrigue machinery came up with more fresh assertions.

Since then twenty years have passed. Much has been put right and corrected. Now that I no longer need fear being thrown into prison or punishment camps for having served Hitler for ten years in his immediate circle, I hope to be able to express freely what I experienced with Hitler, to whom duty-bound I stood closer than anybody with the exception of Eva Braun.

Heinz Linge

Author's Introduction

I N THE MIDST OF the deafening cacophony of exploding Soviet artillery shells, a pistol shot rang out in Adolf Hitler's bunker complex. I did not hear it myself, but as the odour of the gun discharge drifted through the door frame I knew that Hitler had shot himself. I went to Martin Bormann and asked him to accompany me into the Führer's room. I opened the door. On the sofa with its floral cover our 'boss' Adolf Hitler and his bride Eva Hitler née Braun lay slumped in death. Shortly before, Hitler had given me orders as to what I had to do next. I was to take his body out into the open and burn it.

Ten years had passed since the day when I began my service with Hitler and this moment, 1545 hours on 30 April 1945. A whole world lay between the man to whom, as a member of the *SS-Leibstandarte Adolf Hitler*, I had sworn to be faithful unto death, and this corpse which I had now to wrap in a blanket, carry up the dark, narrow bunker stairway, lay in a shell crater, dowse with petrol and set alight. Here then were the extremes of appearances which Hitler offered between 1935 and 1945. The man who had asked my name in Obersalzberg in the summer of 1934 had been a dominant personality exuding a spellbinding charisma to which few were not prey. He embodied sovereign power, total power. The man whom I burnt and interred under a hail of Red Army shells near the Reich Chancellery was a trembling old man, a spent force, feeble, a failure. Like the Reich which he had aimed to bring into an era of unparalleled brilliance and opulence and had become a heap of rubble, he was the disfigured embodiment of his earlier self.

For ten years I lived in Adolf Hitler's immediate vicinity, saw his decisions, which were to have changed the world, mature or fail. I saw Adolf Hitler as only a handful of others knew and experienced him. Besides Eva Braun and Professor Morell, his personal physician, nobody was in a better position than I to observe the physical decline of the Führer. Göring, Goebbels, Himmler and even Martin Bormann never knew Hitler so intimately and in such very private situations as I did.

After my release from Russian captivity what I read in the memoirs of others came to surprise me. Many of the authors recalled incidents allegedly involving themselves with Hitler personally which in reality they had heard from me at FHQ, in the Reich Chancellery or elsewhere, and after Hitler's death had transformed themselves vicariously into the personal eye-witnesses of the events they recounted. That many of the events had not been as they were now retold was known only to myself. Many pieced together stories inaccurately because they misunderstood statements or observations, and drew false conclusions from them. One of the culprits was the historian Wilhelm von Schramm, employed on the Wehrmacht command staff from the French campaign in 1940 until 1943 at OKW (Oberkommando der Wehrmacht) and OKH (Oberkommando des Heeres) and in the last months of the war, who occasionally spoke with me about Hitler. In his book *Der Geheimdienst in Europa, 1937–1945*, von Schramm wrote in 1974:

> At Hitler's FHQ Adlerhorst I learned of the despair of an eye-witness who know the 'Boss' at close hand and the longest – Linge. He was Hitler's personal orderly . . . we often met in the small canteen in the evenings. Linge was always an interesting and above all free conversationalist because he trusted me. Once when we were totally alone he talked to me . . . about Hitler. Quietly he

depicted the condition of the Boss, which since Christmas (1944) was clearly deteriorating . . . Linge no longer believed in Hitler, in the Führer's genius, in the miracle weapons or the saving intuition of the supreme commander. 'He is (he said) just a sick man.'[1]

It is not clear to me how von Schramm can have arrived at this conclusion. The doubts he attributed to me were never mine. How ill, old and spent Hitler was in 1944 I saw daily, but none of this caused my belief in the Führer's genius to waver. Even the secret and open reservations of military men, and some of the old street fighters such as Gauleiter Bohle, who freely admitted to Hitler his belief that the war could not be won, changed nothing for me. In the course of my duties *Geheimdienst* I had the opportunity regularly to read and hear reports originating from Bormann and Himmler from which I gained an insight into the attitudes of many people whom Hitler – at least outwardly – trusted, or used to trust. That these people confessed their loss of faith in Hitler was something I considered to be a matter for themselves to resolve. The interrogations following the Stauffenberg assassination attempt of 20 July 1944 brought to light the extent of the defeatism regarding the military situation and the doubts about Hitler amongst the military leaders and in the Foreign Ministry. Oberstleutnant Günther Smend, adjutant to chief of the army general staff Generaloberst Zeitzler, stated in writing in early August 1944 that he was unaware of Stauffenberg's plans and preparations to remove Hitler, but knew of the negative outlook of military men in decisive positions since Stalingrad. From that time a chasm had opened between the ideas of the general staff and Hitler's orders, he wrote, which prevented a positive stance on the part of the military. He admitted freely that generals Eduard Wagner, Erich Fellgiebel, Adolf Heusinger or Helmuth Stieff – particularly since the evacuation of the Crimea – had expressed sharp criticism of Hitler,

---

1 Wilhelm von Schramm, *Der Geheimdienst in Europa, 1937–1945*, Albert Lancen-Georg Müller Verlag, Munich 1974, p.348.

doubting his ability to win the war and dismissing 'everything as lunacy'. I world have had to have been blind and deaf to have been ignorant of all this.

Since military men and Party bosses took it upon themselves to make diplomatic enquiries as to how I viewed the situation – following remarks made by the Führer – I would either repeat his views or pretend I had no idea what was going on. It was very important for me whenever possible to avoid being drawn into gossip, which was dangerous to everybody. It would have been easy enough to attribute to me something I had neither said nor thought. The carousel of accusations and 'saving one's honour' after 20 July 1944, now known down to the minutest detail, shows clearly how delicately an officer's head was balanced on his shoulders if he could be linked in any way to utterances against Hitler.

Decisive for me as an SS officer was the concept that whatever the circumstances the flag had to be kept flying – something that a host of military men, including Erich von Manstein, the army commander-in-chief since 20 July 1944, had sworn to Hitler's face to do but had not always kept to his word. That the situation on the fronts, the destroyed German cities, the lack of raw materials, weapons and ammunition in no way compelled everybody to the view that the catastrophic end was close and unavoidable is evidenced by the statements of well-known military men such as von Brauchitsch, who set Hitler's genius against the reality.

Even after his death I never stated that it had been clear to me from my intimate knowledge of him in 1944 how it would soon be up with Hitler. On the contrary even in Soviet captivity I acted as if I had been convinced to the last that Hitler's genius would see us through.

As for his relationship with me, an SS officer selected by him for his personal service, Hitler dispensed with the formality which he insisted everybody else should maintain in his presence. He acted towards me in a natural and even familiar manner. Soon there developed something like a purely human contact which not only lightened the burden of my duties but also gave me the chance to observe Hitler's personality.

While Hitler publicly – and even to a certain degree towards his intimate entourage of military men, ministers, women, a few artists and the close colleagues – was ultimately the unapproachable and inscrutable Führer, in my presence he always acted as perhaps he secretly preferred it should be. To me he never postured, was never the 'monument', the statue, which he had made himself from the beginning of his political activity. Often I heard him say things that were not in the programmed script. That I have not made them public until now, in any manner whatever, has been the result of my ideas of loyalty and obedience to my pledge of secrecy with regard to my former post. Additionally, as is the way of things, I knew there was bound to be conflict as soon as I set out my account of certain events and corrected thereby a few memoirs.

Hitler is dead, but at the time of writing (1980) many of his former collaborators who influenced events of the time survive. Many have set out to justify their role in postwar publications with varying degrees of success. Scarcely a general can be found amongst them who admits that he lost a battle by his own bad leadership. The lost war, and all the lost battles, are placed almost exclusively at Hitler's door. It is not for me to judge who made or suggested the right decisions, but I can bear witness that Hitler's predictions in most cases were the right ones, and that his orders to the fronts, based on his own remarks, were frequently ignored or sabotaged.

After 1945 several military leaders boasted that they had – or were famed for having – openly contradicted Hitler and failed to obey him. Thus Egbert Kiese wrote in 1978 about the East Prussian General Dietrich von Saucken, wounded thirteen times, who was summoned before Hitler on 12 March 1945 to receive command of 2. Panzerarmee:

Hitler was seated at the map table, flanked by Generaloberst Guderian, Bormann and an adjutant, when von Saucken entered, one hand resting on his cavalry sabre, monocled, saluting with a slight bow instead of the Hitler salute obligatory since 20 July 1944. This was the equivalent of a rebellion, especially since he had not removed his weapon in the ante-chamber. Guderian, Bormann and the adjutant stared at von Saucken and waited for an outburst of rage from Hitler. Nothing happened. Hitler ignored the general and instructed Guderian curtly to deliver the introductory report. Von Saucken's behaviour was not without its effect. After the report, Hitler embarked on a long statement which commenced with the local command structure. Gauleiter Forster was responsible for Danzig, General von Saucken was his second-in-command except in purely military matters. Von Saucken struck the map table but firmly with the palm of his hand and said: 'Herr Hitler, I do not accept being placed under the orders of a Gauleiter!' Hitler remained silent, sunk at his maps. Guderian and Bormann urged von Saucken to be reasonable: they know that the general's head was on the block, but von Saucken would only repeat: 'I do not accept!' After long seconds Hitler broke the tense silence in a weak voice: 'Very well, then do it alone, Saucken.[2]

I was not there when all this allegedly occurred. General von Saucken, awarded the Diamonds to his Knights Cross by Admiral Dönitz on 8 May 1945 for his service as a loyal commander, was not capable of the kind of conduct depicted. The assertion that he addressed Hitler as 'Herr Hitler' instead of 'Mein Führer', struck the map table with his palm in protest and was still wearing a ceremonial sabre two months before the end of the war as though it were peacetime all show clearly how much reliance may be placed on such second-hand accounts.

2 Egbert Kiese, *Danziger Bucht 1945, Dokumentation einer Katastrophe*, Munich 1978, p.270.

The actual standing orders were described by historian Peter Hoffmann[3] based on a statement by Rittmeister Gerhardt Boldt. Even Generaloberst Guderian had had to surrender his weapons before going in to see the Führer.

> Officers of the army general staff, the front staffs, the Luftwaffe and navy summoned before Hitler [he reported] were required to enter the New Reich Chancellery by the entrance at Voss-Strasse 4 and inside were obliged to show their identity papers. Rittmeister Boldt reported on the procedure which he went through as First Orderly Officer of Generaloberst Guderian when he accompanied him on a regular basis from the beginning of February 1945 for situation conferences at the Reich Chancellery. From the entrance, Guderian, Boldt and Loringhoven had to make long detours to reach Hitler's study because of the heavy bomb damage to the building. At each corridor were SS guards, and to pass them they were obliged to produce their identity papers again and again . . . .In the ante-chamber to Hitler's study Guderian and his escort were received by various SS men in field-grey and had to surrender their weapons. Two of the SS men took away their briefcases for a very thorough search. There was no body search . . . After these formalities the officers were allowed to enter the ante-chamber . . . more SS men in field-grey stood at the door to Hitler's study.

Obviously many people would gladly have argued with Hitler: many risked their necks criticising him behind his back. Hitler read all the SD reports. The attitude of the Dutch, French and captured Poles interested him as much as the morale amongst the German people. If he, as numerous military men alleged after 1945, did not wish to hear or see negative military reports, at least in this respect he wanted to receive the facts. I recall SD reports about remarks

---

3 Peter Hoffmann, *Die Sicherheit des Diktators*, Munich/Zurich 1975, p.242.

by foreign workers who had been given lodgings in July 1944 in my home town of Bremen. These stated quite baldly that the Poles and Dutch hated Hitler and were broken-hearted to learn that the assassination attempt of 20 July 1944 had failed. He was called a 'swine' and a 'rotter' who deserved punishment.

The occasional observation 'If the Führer knew that . . . !' was misplaced, for Hitler found out about, and knew, everything. In general he acted against those who complained if they had any possibility of being effective by virtue of their role in society. Whoever contradicted him openly put his or her own life in jeopardy.

Göring said during the Nuremberg trials that all those who had failed to obey Hitler were under the ground. If anybody dared correct him, Hitler would put him right as if he were a stupid teenager. Even Rommel had to leave a conference with his tail between his legs after making repeated attempts to express a dissenting opinion and being ordered to leave the room.

If somebody had the idea of putting a counter-argument when Hitler spoke about 'God and the World', for example, in one of his much-quoted 'table talks', almost without exception the would-be protester never got any further. Hitler usually sensed exactly what everybody around him was thinking, and he would crush the proposed objection by referring to it as an absurdity in his opening sentences.

How should those of us of no great education challenge him at table when he compared the efficiency of lions and camels and arrived at the conclusion that the carnivorous lion was far less efficient than the camel in the desert, which ate plants and grass. Even the experts allowed themselves to be persuaded on details and circumstances like this in their own specialised disciplines when they actually 'knew better than Hitler', a fact they never dared claim until after his death. There are memoirs by such people whose prior utterances about 'our ingenious Führer' still resound today in my ears. I saw them come and go, and not infrequently I heard what they said and reported to Hitler. Academic historians of standing, who listened in silence and often in astonishment to what the Führer was saying about historical events and how they affected the present, somehow failed to discover until much later that much of it had not only been interpreted with a peculiar slant by Hitler, but was also incorrect.

Towards the end of the war, doubts were voiced occasionally in Hitler's presence regarding the possibility of 'final victory' and the situation at the fronts, but the people who dared make the point had some liberty to state their opinions by virtue of their position. But striking the table with the palm in protest, and 'No, Herr Hitler!' . . . not on your life, never after the death of Hindenburg in 1934.

Equally, guests initially averse to Hitler would often capitulate in the Reich Chancellery, at the Berghof or FHQ, to his personality and suggestive eloquence. I was told spontaneously on a number of occasions afterwards that, despite an initial revulsion towards Hitler, a person had mysteriously fallen under his spell and lost his or her resistance. Many came with every outward appearance of unwillingness and of only being there under protest. Of Hitler, who had summoned them, they had no great opinion or none at all. For them he was an uneducated Austrian upstart from the back streets of Vienna.* Yet like all the others, almost without exception, they departed changed men. Hitler felt and knew this exactly, and his invitations and orders were issued with this in mind.

---

* Hitler was brought up in the Linz area. After the death of his mother in 1907 when he was eighteen he moved to Vienna. (Translators' Note)

Chapter 1

I Join Hitler's Staff:
Elser, the Admired Assassin

J UST ONCE TO BE in the presence of Adolf Hitler, even as a duty, was then the wish of millions. Just once, or should I say, 'so long as everything was going well'. Envy accompanied me when in 1935, to my surprise, the choice fell on me to join Hitler's household. Surprised, for I saw nothing special in myself which would justify such a distinction. I had got my certificate of secondary education, had worked in the construction industry and taken mining training in the hope later of becoming a mining engineer. I joined the Waffen-SS in my home town Bremen in 1933 and after a one-year spell with the unit at Berlin-Lichterfelde, in July or August 1934 with about two dozen comrades I was detached from my unit to the 'Berg' as No. 1 Guard: to Obersalzberg, the country seat of Reich Chancellor Adolf Hitler. Hitler appeared on the Berghof terrain, shook everybody by the hand and asked questions about our private lives. He asked me where I came from and my age. This meeting with Hitler, an idol for us young soldiers, made a deep impression on me.

At the end of 1934 it was arranged that two men from the platoon would be selected for the Reich Chancellery. The selection procedure lasted several days, and finally Otto Meyer and I were chosen from a list of fifty. We reported to SA-Obergruppenführer Wilhelm Brückner, Hitler's chief adjutant, who revealed that we were to be attached to the Führer's personal staff. After a short course at the hotel training school, Pasing near Munich, in January 1935 we served in some of the Reich Chancellery departments under Brückner's tutelage. (In 1936 he published a widely read article about the Führer in his private life.)

Finally we were assigned to our duties in the 'Personal Service of the Führer'. Karl Krause, a manservant from the Reichsmarine who had been with Hitler since 1934 awaited us with our instructions. We three were to share the duties amongst ourselves. Hitler wanted to have one man with him constantly. The second man was to accompany him on his travels. This man had the additional task of ensuring that Hitler's clothing and private rooms were in good order, for which purpose he had a chambermaid at his disposal. The third man was to handle the business arrangements in Hitler's household.

On major occasions, on extended journeys and at Party rallies, the three of us would accompany Hitler. Our apparel had to coincide with his. Everything always had to appear exactly the same. On Party occasions we wore SS uniforms. If Hitler wore a civilian suit, not unusual prewar, then we had to wear one too. Whoever believes that Hitler did not want to appear too obvious for fear of assassination attempts is mistaken. In September 1939 during the Polish campaign he advanced beyond our frontline, and I never saw any sign of anxiety in him. I am convinced, however, that when he emphasised repeatedly for propaganda purposes that he had been 'selected by Providence' for a great, unique, historical mission, he did actually believe it. Rudolf Hess once told me that just before the seizure of power, Hitler, Hess, Heinrich Hoffmann and Julius Schaub were all nearly killed in Hitler's Mercedes due to an error by a lorry driver. Hitler was injured in the face and shoulder but with great composure calmed his co-passengers, still paralysed with shock, with the observation that Providence would not allow him to be killed since he still had a great mission to fulfil. He did not fear attempts on his life, and it was obvious to him that he had to move about freely. When concerns were uttered for his safety he said: 'No German worker is going to do anything to me.' That such an attempt might come from some other sector he seemed to discount, or until 1944 at least. He rejected all obvious safety measures as exaggerated. When during a public meeting at the Berlin Sportspalast the police advised him to enter the hall by a special entrance, because otherwise they could not guarantee his safety, he rejected this brusquely with: 'I am not going in by some back door!' When he undertook private journeys, he forbade his Kripo escort to make a passage for him through the crowd and to shield him. He believed and often stated that 'Providence' protected him and that the mere presence of the SS bodyguard was sufficient to dissuade all would-be assassins. What engaged his thoughts more was the possibility of an attempt from abroad to remove him by force. Political fanatics were also to be found in the Reich, he said once, so that he had to live with the possibility of surprises in this respect too. All the same, he was not especially concerned about who was around him and his 'court'. He knew the people at the Berghof by sight but only a few of them by name and employment. It was the same at FHQs. After moving in he would do the rounds, have the various commanders presented to him and content himself with that.

After my release from Russia I was surprised to see the assertion still hawked today that it had been almost impossible to get close enough to Hitler to murder him. This is incorrect. Whoever had cunning, skill and determination could have assassinated Hitler on any one of very many occasions. Often, and not only before the war, people approached him without anybody intervening. Photographers and cameraman dragged into his presence cases of equipment, cables, tripods and film materials, took photographs of him with telescopic lenses and generally moved about freely and unhindered. After the July 1944 bomb plot when preparing to be driven to the military hospital at Rastenburg, he was suddenly surrounded by a large crowd of soldiers and police. Any of them could have killed him had they been so inclined. Although still suffering from wounds to his head and legs from the bomb he was so unmoved by it all that I became anxious for his safety and only relaxed when we finally drove off. Sitting behind him, I could at least protect his back. Admittedly, anyone who wanted to remove Hitler 'eye to eye' would have had to sacrifice his own life. This kind of suicide mission found no takers and was probably the only reason that Hitler survived to die by his own hand in April 1945.

Only very few of the attempts on Hitler's life are known publicly. Some he escaped very closely. After the marriage of Generalfeldmarschall von Blomberg, Hitler drove to Kaiser Wilhelm II's former mansion and hunting range on the Schorfheide to be with Göring. Himmler drove ahead of us. Suddenly shots cracked out from the forest undergrowth. Himmler's car stopped after being hit. Himmler, deeply shocked and pale, told Hitler that he had been shot at. Driving on after the incident, Hitler said: 'That was certainly intended for me because Himmler does not usually drive ahead. It is also well known that I always sit at the side of the driver. The hits on Himmler's car are in that area.' The result was that Hitler's cars were given armour plating.

Shortly before the war an adjutant accepted for Hitler a bouquet of roses from the crowd. After the adjutant reported the sudden onset of a mysterious illness the bouquet was examined and it was found that the thorns had been treated with poison. This 'flower attempt' had as its consequence a ruling that flowers and other objects had to be handled in future only when wearing gloves. Later the tossing of flowers into Hitler's car was in general forbidden. One day, dog-lover Hitler was given a dog as a present. The animal had been infuriated in some way, but this was detected when it bit one of the escort. Hitler was always lucky (except for his injuries on 20 July 1944) but early on had gradually become more cautious. Foods from abroad could not be eaten in the household. Despite this prohibition, in 1944 I had not been able to resist the temptation to taste a gift of fruit. The result was a bout of poisoning diagnosed by Dr Morell, Hitler's personal physician, which kept me in bed for weeks. Hitler was examined daily by his doctor while Reichsleiter Albert Bormann was ordered to test not only all food but also the water daily.

The first attempt on Hitler's life to become widely known and arouse excitement worldwide occurred in Munich in 1939. In the so-called 'Capital of the Movement' on the eve of the commemoration of the march to the Feldherrnhalle of 9 November 1923, a reunion of the *Alte Kämpfer* was scheduled in the Bürgerbräukeller. Hitler was to take part as usual. The war was two months old and Hitler, who needed to be in Berlin on the morning of 9 November, arranged for the reunion to begin early and cancelled his usual meeting with old comrades. This decision saved his life.

The following communiqué was published in the German Press on 9 November 1939:

> On Wednesday (8 November) the Führer made a brief visit to Munich for the commemoration celebrations of the Alte Kämpfer. The Führer himself delivered the address in the Bürgerbräukeller in place of Party member Hess. Since affairs of state required the attendance of the Führer in Berlin that night, he left the Bürgerbräukeller earlier than originally planned and boarded the waiting train at the main station. Shortly after the Führer's departure an explosion occurred in the Bürgerbräukeller. Of those still present in the room seven were killed and sixty-three injured. The assassination attempt, which by its traces appears to have been a foreign plot, caused immediate great outrage in Munich. A reward of 500,000 RM has been offered for the arrest and conviction of the perpetrators, and a further 600,000 RM from private sources. The devastating explosion in the Bürgerbräukeller occurred at about 2120 hours, at a time when the Führer had already left the hall. Nearly all leaders of the Movement, Reichsleiters and Gauleiters, had accompanied him to the railway station, where he boarded the

train for his return to Berlin on urgent state business immediately after concluding his address. One must consider it a miracle that the Führer escaped the attempt with his life. The attempt was a blow struck against the security of the Reich.[1]

A fortnight later it was announced that thirty-six-year-old Johann Georg Elser had been arrested shortly after the attempt while trying to cross the frontier into Switzerland. He was said to have been the man who placed the bomb in the Bürgerbräukeller about 145 hours before the explosion. I was with Hitler when Himmler delivered his report. Elser, born 4 January 1903 at Hermaringen/Württemberg as the illegitimate son of a heavy drinker of the locality, a wood merchant by the name of L. Elser, had confessed his intention to kill Hitler. According to Himmler's statement, Elser was 'no carbon copy of the Reichstag arsonist van der Lubbe'. Elser had declared that he alone knew of his preparations for the attempt and nobody had put him up to it. When Himmler said that in his statement Elser admitted to being obsessed by the idea of having his photograph in the newspapers, Hitler asked for a photograph to be produced.

The man had admitted wanting to be a 'Herostratos of the present',[*] Himmler went on. Hitler, who was studying the photograph, listened at first with a granite face, then said slowly: 'Himmler, that does not seem right. Just look at the physiognomy, the eyes, the intelligent features. This is no seducer of men, no chatterer. He knows what he wants. Find out what political circles are behind him. He may be a loner, but he does not lack a political point of view.' Himmler made a surprised face and assured Hitler that his

---

1 Translation of the DNB (Deutsche Nachrichten Büro) text of 9 November 1939.

* In 356 Herostratus went on a murderous rampage and burnt down the Temple to Artemis at Ephesus. This was his revolt against egalitarianism, to make his mark on history even at the price of becoming infamous. (TN)

people would soon find out 'whose spiritual child' the would-be assassin was.

Elser interested Hitler in an odd way. The man whose philosophy in the Ernst Röhm affair and elsewhere was to 'kill, shovel out the shit', reacted to Elser quite differently. When he saw Himmler's mystified expression he said under his breath: 'I am allowing him to live only so that he knows I am right and he is wrong.' Himmler, disconcerted, went off to make his further enquiries. Soon afterwards Hitler received details about Elser's career. As the eldest of five children he had left school in 1917 to train as a turner in an iron foundry at Königsbronn, but gave this up to train in carpentry, qualifying two years later. The best of his class in 1922, he considered himself an 'artistic carpenter' and experimented with ideas involving clocks, motors and locks. Next Elser obtained employment at Dornier's Friedrichshafen aircraft works in the propeller section for three to four years, where he was a good worker. He went on to spend a year in a clock factory where he proved sociable, was a good zither and double-bass musician and had various affairs with women.

All this reinforced Hitler's original impression, and he reproached Himmler: 'Herostratus? Just look – member of the Woodworkers' Union, member of the Red Front Fighters' League and a churchgoer – and no political motive? How could he make anybody believe that?' Hitler had completed his assessment of Elser and ordered Himmler to get Elser to build another bomb. Elser obliged. 'This man's abilities,' Hitler said in recognition of them, 'could be useful in wartime, blowing up bridges and suchlike. Give him a workshop in a prison or concentration camp where he can continue his bomb-making activities.'

As a 'special detainee' (*Sonderhäftling*) at Sachsenhausen concentration camp Elser was grouped together with Léon Blum, Kurt von Schussnigg, Pastor Niemöller and a number of other well-known personalities and worked for years on the task Hitler had given him. He invented, designed and built bombs to Hitler's order.

Hitler suspended the criminal proceedings against him, something that may have surprised the public. It is alleged occasionally that Hitler knew in advance of a bomb having been placed in the Bürgerbräukeller, and this was the reason why he had arrived and left earlier than planned. For my own part I knew Hitler's reactions and was able to tell reliably from his composure if he were genuinely surprised or just pretending, and it was my opinion in November 1939 that he had no foreknowledge.

I guessed that within his trusted circle Hitler had no desire to speak of his frustration at the British response to the invasion of Poland. A number of the Party bosses, the Gauleiter Rudolf Hess, Goebbels (who accompanied Hitler to Berlin) and others might have spoken privately at the Bürgerbräukeller of his prophecy about Britain's 'friendly' attitude to the Reich. This would certainly not have pleased him. According to Himmler, Elser had done no harm to Hitler, had expressly recanted, admitted his guilt and changed his outlook at Sachsenhausen. He told several people there that the Gestapo paid him 40,000 Swiss francs to plant the bomb and set the timer for the hour they wanted. I never dared broach this subject with Hitler. When the official police bulletin on 16 April 1945 reported the death of Elser the previous day in an Allied bombing raid, a somewhat noteworthy occurrence, I had other matters to concern me. Defeat was at hand.

Hitler's composure on the day of the assassination attempt and the fact that Elser would have had to spend all day in the Bürgerbräukeller undiscovered near the column where he had put the bomb seem noteworthy in retrospect, bearing in mind how Himmler's security organisation automatically made its screening preparations for meetings of this kind. In my opinion Hitler's reaction after the attempt was not feigned: it seemed too original, too spontaneous. At that time I would not have believed it possible of him to risk the lives of the Alte Kämpfer without betraying himself in some way.

A lot about the Elser case was extraordinary. That Hitler allowed Elser to go on living because, as he informed Himmler, his inventive abilities could be useful in the war, seemed very questionable to me in 1939, for our experts were in no need of a clockmaker/carpenter to provide them with ideas. I had the impression that Hitler admired Elser's quiet dedication and constancy. Elser was basically a man whom he would have liked to have seen active in the SS, SA or the Party. Elser, the 'simple worker' as Hitler once called him, had the courage at the end of 1939 to do something for his 'political world-view' when German generals opposed to Hitler had merely resigned. Hitler, who drew attention to himself in *Mein Kampf* and in public speeches as having once been a 'simple worker', was always more impressed by special achievements from this level than by corresponding efforts of the so-called 'higher-ups'. He was convinced that the workforce belonged to him 'heart and hand'. More than once he said that he would lay his head to sleep in the lap of any German worker without the least fear. He never accepted that the workers only followed him because he gave them work and bread after years of despair, as is often maintained nowadays.

The Elser case was something special for him without a doubt. Since the Nuremberg trials we have come to understand how the lives of people in Hitler's Germany counted for very little. This can be confirmed by reading the death sentences from that time. Thus we have a mystery how Elser, whom Hitler ought to have wanted dead, stayed alive almost to the end when the men and women around Graf von Stauffenberg in 1944 were hanged like cattle. Workers who went through thick and thin to 'follow the mismanaged nobility' were also lost to Hitler in principle, while Thälmann the German communist leader and Elser were for him 'men of character' in whom he saw much to be admired. It seems to me that this aspect of his personality lacks research. I read often after the war that Hitler was so fearful of assassination attempts he always had the window blinds let down when he travelled by train. This was not the reason: his eyes were intolerant of sunlight. Even bright artificial light hurt them and accordingly his headwear always had a large brim, or peak worn low. Heinrich Hoffmann, his personal photographer, had to succeed with the first few flashbulbs or abandon their use. On Obersalzberg before the war a large tree was planted on the spot where Hitler took march-pasts in summer. Since he wanted to appear bare-headed without a sun canopy, and the tree was the only way.

Chapter 2

Hitler the Architect

A FTER OTTO MEYER[1] AND Karl Krause[2] had been dismissed by Hitler in April 1938 and during the Polish campaign, respectively, and returned to their units, the field was left to me, a person of few words, reserved and dour, to slip automatically into a position that extended well beyond my original employment as Hitler's butler. In the course of time I was entrusted with ever more responsibilities, and by the end of July 1944 with the rank of SS-Hauptsturmführer[3] was finally Head of the Personal Service to the Führer.[4] In this role I had to be in constant attendance to Hitler, accompany him on his travels and be responsible for the maintenance of his accommodation. The servants, officers' mess orderlies, Hitler's caterers and everybody whose duties were in some way concerned with Hitler's care were subordinated to me.

---

1 Meyer was required to leave because he gave relatives theatre boxes reserved for the Führer's guests.

2 Hitler, who feared being given poisoned water following reports during the campaign that Poles were contaminating water sources, had ordered that he be served only Fachinger mineral water. Krause served him water, falsely stating that it was Fachinger. When he was unable to produce the bottle at Hitler's request, he had to go.

3 SS-Hauptsturmführer = army rank of captain.

4 Hans Junge was Linge's deputy until 1942 when he was transferred to the front. Next came Eugen Bussmann, but he proved a constant source of annoyance to Hitler and at Linge's suggestion was transferred to the SS-Führerbegleitkommando, Hitler's bodyguard.

When taking up a new post, one obviously keeps one's eyes and ears open. I made cautious enquiries to determine what was important and unimportant. It was important, as I quickly learned, to observe the demarcation lines between the individual members of 'court': 'Everything else', I was informed, 'you have to find out for yourself.' And so it was. Whenever somebody mentioned anything personal about the Führer I had to be alert to it, for this was my work territory. Hitler, a master in 'selling himself', encouraged me to 'come out of my shell' and so smoothed the way for me that I quickly lost all the shyness which had intimidated me not only in my relations with him but also with other important Reich celebrities.

That I should expect surprises day in, day out went with the job, for beyond his stereotyped customs Hitler could act unpredictably. Erich Kempka's predecessor Julius Schreck told me about an incident involving Hitler which illustrated the type of thing that could occur. Schreck was driving Hitler to the Pfalz in the Mercedes with the usual convoy following. On a main highway they passed two RAD[5] youths walking to the next town. They thumbed a lift, not realising who was in the Mercedes. Hitler told Schreck to stop and called the two youths over. 'Their eyes nearly popped out,' Schreck said, 'here in the middle of nowhere, the Führer.' Hitler invited them to climb in and chatted with them as they drove. When dropping the pair off Hitler mentioned that it looked like rain, they should keep their capes handy. One replied that he had been unemployed so long he had not been able to afford one. At once Hitler put his own trenchcoat over the boy's shoulders and drove on. For those present it was an effective propaganda event shortly after the seizure of power, but for those responsible for Hitler's wardrobe it was a cause for annoyance. A new coat had to be procured quickly. It had to look like the last one, fit him and be available immediately. I realised that if possible I should always have with me at all times on these travels spectacles,

---

5 RAD = Reichs Arbeits Dienst, the six-month period of compulsory communal work service.

magnifying glasses, colour writing implements and writing utensils, spare shoes, boots, socks, uniform trousers, ties, shirts, gloves, caps and hats for any emergency.

Visitors often told me that it took their breath away when Hitler looked them in the eyes. He never had this effect on me, however. His eyes, described thousands of times as 'weird', fascinating, even hypnotising, never impressed me. Obviously I could not look away any time he happened to fix his gaze on me but I was never 'transfixed'. To the frequently asked question what 'the thing' was that compelled everybody to kowtow to Hitler, I have to say I have no idea. He was my boss. I cannot even say the boss of my boss, for I had no other. Nobody, not even Himmler or Bormann, was authorised to give me orders. That, and simply his personality, bound me to *him*, not to a world-political view or idea. Ministers, generals and high-up NSDAP functionaries related to me Hitler's uncommon abilities, knowledge and leadership qualities. What he knew and could do was something I could not judge. My orders were simply to listen out for what the generally acknowledged experts said having regard to events worldwide; I was to do no more than watch how they behaved in Hitler's presence. Yet how could I not have believed Hitler a genius and unique when every day I saw and heard how the major personalities of the Reich fawned over him and worshipped him with total devotion.

Even though he had already been Reich Chancellor for the past two years, when I began my service with Hitler in 1935 he was still living on Obersalzberg in his old country house, Haus Wachenfeld, which was both small and rather primitive. The winter-garden, for example, where the meals were served, was so cramped that guests had to stack up the crockery after eating to help the orderlies because of the lack of space. If Göring put in a surprise appearance, the other guests had to huddle closer together at table because he took up two places.

Wilhelm Brückner, by whom I was 'taught' in 1935, wrote the following year in his essay on Hitler's private life:

> Many people wonder why the Führer chose Obersalzberg for his home. Whoever has stood up there realises that there is probably no other place in Germany from where, despite the nearness of the surrounding mountains, one has such a wide and unobstructed view of the world's beauty. In a section of the mountains to the north, at the foot of the Gaisberg, lies the old bishopric city of Salzburg. On days when the strong Alpine south wind known as the Föhn blows, one can see the city with the naked eye . . . left of Obersalzberg towers the Untersberg Massif . . . farther left the gaze wanders to the Watzmann and the giant mountains surrounding it which come round in a wide arc and peak behind Obersalzberg in the Hohe Göll . . . here, amidst this hugeness of Nature . . . lives the Führer, where he works on his great speeches.

I often noticed that the surrounding mountains inspired Hitler. He once joked that here he stood 'above the world' in an environment comparable to Olympus, legendary mount of the gods, but that alone can never have been the motivation for him to put down his private roots on Obersalzberg. Often in quieter moments another reason would surface: the memory of his friend and mentor Dietrich Eckart. Here, not far from the 'little house on the Göll' in which the Bavarian writer, poet and dramatist had lived prior to his death, Hitler would often reminisce. Frequently he would remind me of the hero Antaios[6] of Greek legend, who created new energy from his contact with the earth.

That Hitler did not envisage Obersalzberg as his 'eternal' abode is clear from his intention, more often expressed the longer the war went on, to retire eventually to Linz. But as long as he used the

---

6 In Greek mythology Antaios (Antaeus), son of Poseidon and the Earth goddess Gaia, was a wrestler who drew his invincible strength from the Earth.

Berghof – and he was still calculating in 1944 how he would need it until 1949 – he regarded himself as domiciled there.

He had Haus Wachenfeld rebuilt to his own plans. On the first floor of the rebuilt Berghof were his study and the bedrooms for Eva Braun and himself. There were twelve other guest rooms for visitors. The permanent house-staff lived in, near the guests. All rooms had valuable paintings on the walls: originals such as those by von Lenbach, Defregger, Grützner, Waldmüller, Spitzweg, Stuck, Titian and Makart were Hitler's favourites. In the basement was his 'sports centre', a bowling alley. Hitler, who had no interest in sport except for the expander under his bed, loved bowling, although he did not want this known about. 'If the bowling associations get wind of it', he said, 'they will make me honorary president of every club.'

The Berghof terrain had a private tea-house, Mooslahner Kopf, which Hitler the rambler visited almost every afternoon in peace time. Some 800 metres above the Mooslahner Kopf, on the Kehlstein, was the world-famous second tea-house. The idea for this construction, which to my recollection cost about 30 million RM, came from Martin Bormann. From the Berghof at an altitude of 1,000 metres a road led through a tunnel to a parking place at 1,700 metres. From here at the end of a gallery 130 metres long was a lift which rose up 120 metres through the rock of the mountain to the tea-house entrance. Hitler visited it only when he had special guests on the Berghof, such as the crown princess of Italy, Mussolini and André François-Poncet. When the last ascended with Hitler's personal adjutant, Brückner remarked: 'Your Excellency, now we are rising into hell.' With a laugh, François-Poncet replied: 'No, into heaven'. The rooms of this Kehlsteinhaus as it was called were not large, and the only ones worthy of note were the dining room and large circular Fireplace Room, which provided a wonderful view of the glorious mountain scenery.

Martin Bormann, administrator of the NSDAP-owned Obersalzberg, was responsible not only for the maintenance of the properties and installations but also for any changes to the zone of the so-called Führer-terrain. On his instructions, from Party funds, barracks, guesthouses, a Bormann-administered farm and country houses for Göring, Speer and himself were erected. Hitler, keen on architecture and even in 1945 still 'dreaming' of designs which he was hoping to get built at some future time, let Bormann have his head in his fury of building but joked of him: 'This is a mole which moves mountains overnight', an observation not far from the truth.

In 1938 in Bormann's presence, Hitler happened to mention that a farmyard not far from the Berghof did not harmonise with the scenery. Nothing more. When he returned from a short stay in Munich a few days later he could hardly believe his eyes. Red cattle were grazing the field where the day before the farmhouse and yard had stood. Bormann had bought it, relocated the owners, had the buildings dismantled by hundreds of construction workers and had returfed the area. Hitler had misgivings, however, that the owner had not sold his property so 'willingly' and 'voluntarily' as Bormann had described in response to his enquiry, and in my presence he spoke of his doubts and even hinted at an abuse of power.

Before the war I often had the impression of being in the household of a busy architect and building tycoon rather than the Führer and Reich Chancellor. Sketches of buildings, outline plans, calculations, designs of all kinds, draughtsmen's implements, coloured pencils and architectural utensils were always on his table, and Hitler worked there endlessly, changing and correcting designs, consulting technical books and making comparisons. Occasionally he would talk with me, the trainee civil engineer who had done construction work, about the life of the building worker, the plumber and the carpenter. I was surprised at the depth of his knowledge in the details of the artisan's work. Whenever I looked at his cared-for hands I found it hard to believe his assertion that he had worked for a while on a building site. What he wrote about this in *Mein Kampf* I read only ten years after the war. Until then I knew his book only by its cover. He never asked me if I had read it or possessed a copy. I know today that he made mention of an incident after the death of his mother[7] when he had been ejected from a property in Vienna by social-democrat building workers for arguing about politics and contradicting their opinions. Only after reading *Mein Kampf* did I realise in retrospect how on visits to construction sites he would ask questions so knowledgeable that I would not know where to start for an answer. The deplorable monotony which he had experienced on the site in Vienna remained fixed in his memory.

Hitler often said that if Providence had not decided he should be Führer of the German people, he would certainly have been a leading figure in the field of architecture which, as he liked to emphasise, would have spared him the cares and worries which now confronted him constantly. I noticed his eagerness to oversee and urge forward all the costliest, and in his view most important, building projects. Yes, he even became involved personally on decisive designs, models and changes, and took over from the architects Hermann Giesler and Albert Speer, two of the most important of them, who brought his plans and ideas to fruition, organised the builders and regulated the financial side. He urged, insisted on haste and – even during the war – tolerated delays with bad grace. Many structures arose, as it were, almost overnight.

The New Reich Chancellery had to be finished and commissioned in 1938 within nine months. At the end of January 1938 Speer received the order from Hitler to begin the work immediately. This caught Speer on the hop, for although he had been asked to work on the plans to enlarge the Reich Chancellery three years earlier, the instruction to get started straight away was unexpected. Within eight weeks the older structure had been pulled down and the site from the Wilhelm-Platz to Friedrich-Ebert-Strasse along the Voss-Strasse prepared so that the project could begin. On 2 August 1938

---

7 Hitler's mother died at Urfahr, Linz on 21 December 1907.

'we' and about 8,000 building workers and employees in Berlin and the Gau districts throughout the Reich celebrated the completion of the work, and on 12 January 1939 Hitler received the Diplomatic Corps in the new building and dedicated it.

Almost overnight as I said, many buildings sprang up. This was one of them. Within a few months 420 rooms totalling 360,000 cubic metres in volume stood on 16,300 square metres of ground. Twenty million bricks were used: faced with shell limestone for the 120 metre by 22.2 metre central section, where the great reception rooms were situated, and with Jura dolomite for the sixty-eight metre by twenty-six metre Ehrenhof. The walls, fourteen metres high in the Round Hall, were dressed overall in marble.

The Führer's study was clad in dark red Limbach marble. It was 9.75 metres high and had a surface area of 27 metres by 14.5 metres. A passage 146 metres long, 9.5 metres high and 12 metres in width, much admired by Hitler, led to his study from the domed Round Hall. Since I had been present at the building work from its inception I observed it all with the greatest interest. At least I never heard from Hitler what I had had to listen to over and again as an apprentice civil engineer: he never spoke of the costs which would be in the region of 380 million DM at today's (1980) prices. His mind was only on the architecture, which played a central role in his cultural politics and was a symbol for the vitality of the new Reich and belief in its future. All this building work also served the ends of propaganda and made the Third Reich appear to be in the throes of expansion. In the grounds (421 metres by 402 metres) a magnificent garden had been laid to include the old park in which Otto von Bismarck used to stroll. His portrait by Lenbach hung above Hitler's marble fireplace in the study.

Hitler did not have a normal relationship with money, the management of which he left entirely in the hands of Brückner, his chief adjutant. The budget that he received as Reich Chancellor was just sufficient, in his opinion, as he very often informed us, to maintain his SS bodyguard. The 'State-at-Court' in his Führer-HQs he covered with royalties from *Mein Kampf*. As he always had considerable sums to his credit at Franz-Eher-Verlag his publisher – in 1944 seven or eight million RM[8] – he was very generous and I would often hear him ask Brückner for a statement of the balance. If he received a satisfactory reply he would send sums to organisations such as Mother and Child, National Socialist Welfare or youth institutions. Then he would say as if relieved: 'Now it's all gone again, and I have peace of mind.' Whoever heard that might infer that Hitler felt oppressed by money. The fact is that he felt guilty in some way that people went without because they were short of cash.

He paid his closest staff handsomely. 'My people', he remarked once, 'have a standard of living with me which I consider the correct one. Working at my side they should have an adequate income. Nobody should have to succumb to temptation, allow themselves to be corrupted or engage in unfair practices for need of money. If they do, I reserve the right in such cases to punish harshly and pitilessly.' And he did so. When two orderlies stole paintings and artistic models from his display of birthday presents they were sent to a concentration camp. He occasionally threatened others openly with immediate transfer to a camp, and this always had the desired effect.

In this regard I would like to mention an incident in Berlin before the war. A torrential downpour had flooded the lower rooms of the Old Reich Chancellery, including the Führer apartments. Everything was 'afloat'. Carpets, papers and other objects were soaked and ruined. Even worse, the sewage rose and mixed with the filthy water in the rooms causing a bestial stink. How the important papers were restored later I have no idea. I was glad that I had nothing to do with it. To aggravate matters, the Polish minister, Beck, called at the Reich Chancellery. The visitors had to climb the steps to reach

---

8 See Werner Maser (ed.), *Adolf Hitler: Mein Kampf*, Esslingen 1974, p.39.

the drier levels. Hitler was raging. He summoned the responsible architect and asked him how such a thing could have occurred. It was explained that Berlin's water table was too high and the pumps had not been adequate to deal with the rainwater. Hitler wanted to know next if the surrounding buildings had also flooded. Enquiries showed that this had not been the case. Incensed, Hitler ordered that plans to overcome the problem in the Old Reich Chancellery should be drawn up as soon as possible. When the architect and his staff returned with plans and files and informed Hitler that improvements were not possible, he frowned and tightened his lips. I was standing near him, recognised the signs and tensed for an outburst. Instead he spoke in an undertone whose menace was unmistakable: '*Meine Herren*, if you have not rid us of this problem within the shortest possible time, I shall have you all sent forthwith to a concentration camp. I hope you understand me.' Then he turned and walked off. The specialists looked at each other appalled, then left the room with their tails between their legs. So long as they were in earshot I heard no word spoken by them. Hitler's anger at the 'hollow-heads' and 'bunglers' who could not even cure 'minor things like that' was not forgotten so quickly by them, but at least the Old Reich Chancellery never flooded again.

Whether we were in Berlin, Munich or at the Berghof, architecture was always Hitler's most intense pastime. He had already started work on Munich, the so-called Capital of the Movement, when the plans for Berlin were still to some extent in the design stage. In 1935 when Albert Speer began planning the rebuilding of the Reich Chancellery, Hitler had already laid the foundation stone for the representative House of German Art in Munich in October 1933, and by 1937 had completed the most important work on the Königs-Platz.

Augsburg, Bayreuth, Berlin, Breslau, Dresden, Düsseldorf, Graz, Hamburg, Linz, Munich, Münster, Oldenburg, Posen, Nuremberg, Duisburg, Saarbrücken, Hanover, Cologne, Innsbruck,

Königsberg, Stettin, Weimar and Würzburg were all declared by Hitler to be cities for remodelling. Danzig, Wuppertal, Bremen and Memel were added at the beginning of 1941. Such projects, which often originated from Hitler, were sometimes of such a dimension as to defy imagination. Barracks were built, autobahns and ring roads laid, airports established. The whole Reich was the drawing board for the Lord of the Architects, and to make things worse he fanned the flames of jealousies and quarrels within the guild of architects. This one wanted to be 'the Führer's preferred architect', that one 'the Führer's personal architect'. Disputes over nebulous areas of jurisdiction and demarcation lines became the order of the day. After the war a picture of all this emerged which was not entirely accurate.

After my return from captivity I was surprised to find that the only architect there had ever been in the Third Reich was Albert Speer. Speer's own publications after his release from Spandau fostered this impression further. Certainly, Speer had been 'Generalbauinspektor' for Berlin. Yet Paul Ludwig Troost and Hermann Giesler were both 'Generalbaurat' for Munich, the Capital of the Movement (from December 1938); for Weimar, Roderick Fick (from December 1938); Ludwig and Franz Ruff – alongside Speer – for the Nuremberg Rally structures; and Brugmann and Schmeisser for the city plans. Fick and Dr Fritz Todt designed and built the Obersalzberg to Hitler's ideas. Reissinger planned the Gau installations at Bayreuth; architect Kreis the new city centre at Dresden; Dipl-Ing Peter Koller the city rebuilding at Graz and Innsbruck; Konstanty Gutschow the Hamburg Gauhaus; architect Bartels the city centre at Münster and the Gau complex; and so on. Bangert and Schmidt were competent for Posen, Claassen for Stettin, Gross for Würzburg, Mehrtens for Frankfurt an der Oder. What they planned and built was guided by the hand and spirit of the frustrated architect Adolf Hitler.

In May 1938 – we had recently returned from Italy and Hitler had just nominated a Gauleiter for the newly created Alps-and-

Danube Gau – columns of workers began work on the Munich underground railway and tramway systems. Hitler, who had long been pressing for the work to go ahead, attended the commencement of the subway project at the Goethe-Platz station. After much of the new construction had been taken in hand and partially realised in Munich, from 1933 onwards, there then began, so Hitler insisted, 'the greatest work for the expansion and beautification of this city'. The job was to be finished by 1944 at the latest.

I was not the only person to be seized by great enthusiasm. I believed we were on the road to great times. We hoped that what Hitler had announced to the Munich subway workers in his address of 22 May 1938 would come to pass:

> The city will receive an exemplary network of fast tramways which will connect the outskirts with the city centre. It will then be possible within a few years to extend the tramway out of the city centre. . . . At the latest in five to six years this work will be finally concluded. Munich will then have an outstanding traffic network for rapid mass transit and above all a series of major rail installations with a new large central station as its hub. What happens here will be repeated in Berlin, and I hope that both cities will enter into a noble rivalry in the sense that each tries to outdo the other in the knowledge of what is necessary. The solution to traffic problems is the major reason for the great projects which have been taken in hand especially in Berlin, Munich and Hamburg.[9]

That it might not go to plan I considered impossible in 1938, and so for my own personal considerations I interested myself in what Hitler was attempting to achieve with all this civil planning. What he said bred in me wonderful hopes, and already I could picture

---

9 Max Domarus, *Hitler, Reden und Proklamationen, 1932–1945*, Munich 1965, vols I and II, p.865.

myself as a civil engineer of standing and of course 'not badly off'. Hitler declared:

> We want these projects to be completed in the spirit of the age. Our time is governed by our concerns for the future of the German people. I hope that these projects which we complete today will prove amply large for the centuries ahead. A couple of statistics show that our ancestors had an equally broad concept. When the street Unter den Linden was built in the seventeenth century, Berlin had only 40,000 inhabitants, and when Ludwig-Strasse in Munich was built Munich had a population of only 70,000. Munich today has over 800,000 and Berlin more than 4.5 million inhabitants. For that reason nobody should come to me and say our new streets are being built too broad . . . As we embark upon this enormous task, we recognise once more that everything is only possible because the concentrated strength of a people 75 million strong stands behind it. Berlin does not build Berlin, Hamburg does not build Hamburg, Munich does not build Munich and Nuremberg does not build Nuremberg, but Germany builds for itself its cities, its beautiful, its proud, its glorious cities.[10]

Albert Speer, of whom much was predicted on Obersalzberg, was assessed by us all as an objective and clever man, far-sighted and sure-footed in his political instincts. He wrote in 1936 that:

> . . . the Führer's great structures, which today are beginning to mushroom at many locations, will be an expression of the spirit of the Movement for millennia and a part themselves of the Movement . . . he builds as a National Socialist. As such he determines, just as he does the will and expression of the Movement, the neatness and purity of architectural design . . . It will be unique in the

10 Max Domarus, *Hitler, Reden und Proklamationen, 1932–1945*, Munich 1965, vols I and II, p.865.

history of the German people that its leader has begun a decisive change not only with the greatest world-political New Order in our history but is, with his superior architectural knowledge, creating simultaneously those structures in stone which, in millennia, will continue to bear witness to the political will and cultural knowledge of this great era.

Dr Fritz Todt, who knew that I had worked in construction before I came to the Führer, recalled with enthusiasm how on 23 September 1933 Hitler had opened a stretch of autobahn between Frankfurt and Darmstadt which had been planned for years. Full of hope, 700 formerly unemployed workers direct from the labour exchanges marched to Frankfurt's Börsen-Platz where the Gauleiters handed them their work tools. To music they then proceeded to a street construction site where countless men, women and children waited expectantly. Before them that morning Hitler appeared, his drive through Frankfurt having a carnival atmosphere. Todt knew the closing phrases of Hitler's speech by heart. 'Now go to work!' Hitler said, and continued: 'The building work must begin today. Let work commence! Before years have passed, this gigantic work will bear witness to our will, our industry, our ability and our determination. German workers, to the work!' Then, according to Todt, something happened which fascinated and charmed everybody. Hitler went up to the first soil-laden truck, took a spade and repeated: 'To the work! Let's begin!' Together with two workers he began shovelling out all the earth from the truck. Some 700 workers watched him do it. Their thoughts are not difficult to guess. Their response showed it. By the end of September they had taken home the greater part of this 'Hitler-earth' in their pockets and bags.

Chapter 3

Hitler on Diet and the Evils of Smoking

UNTIL 1944 I LOOKED to the future with optimism. In case I could not work as a civil engineer later by reason of the time I had lost through my employment with Hitler, my future was nevertheless well provided for. As I perceived the situation after July 1944, Frederick the Great, with whom Hitler liked to be compared, had given Johann Friedrich von Domhardt (who held approximately the same office with the great Prussian king as I had with Hitler) a directorship in East Prussia, the presidency of the War and Domains Chamber at Gumbinnen and the senior presidency of East and West Prussia. If I, who since the Stauffenberg plot of 20 July 1944 had been Hitler's constant travel companion and table guest at Table One, chief of the Personal Service to the Führer and with it 'Lord of the Service Personnel and the Personal Care of Hitler', could not cherish such hopes – and Hitler doubtless had other ideas than Frederick the Great in this respect – I was nevertheless convinced that, after evacuating my post when the time came to step aside, my nest would be well feathered thanks to Hitler, and I could expect to lead a reasonably care-free life. Hitler told Himmler at the end of 1944: 'After the war, Linge will be Marshall of Travel and Court'.

Life in Hitler's immediate environment was no bed of roses. Not without cause did I request him on a number of occasions to release me for the front. Even the spartan Generaloberst Alfred Jodl often complained during the war: 'My God, life in a concentration camp cannot be much more exhausting and depressing than here.'

How much he was deceived in this he was to discover during the Nuremberg trials, when he was sentenced to hang in 1946.

As everywhere, Hitler set himself up as the yardstick. If a stranger to FHQ Wolfsschanze did not know better and saw Hitler's bedroom with its military-issue field bed, he would have thought it to be the dormitory of a subaltern. After having had the opportunity to peer briefly behind the scenes and shaking his head in amazement, Generalfeldmarschall von Bock once said to me: 'Our infantry at the front should see this.' Occasionally Hitler shocked me too, although over the course of time I became inured to most surprises. Early one morning upon returning from an 'excursion' and creeping past Hitler's bedroom, I heard a sort of grinding noise within. It was so unusual that I entered. I gasped. Hitler was standing barefoot in his nightshirt attempting to change the light bulb in the ceiling, a procedure he found very difficult because of the nerve damage to his arm. I apologised and asked: 'Mein Führer, why did you not call me?' He looked at me and replied: 'Should I wake you up just to change a light bulb? I can do it myself, as you can see.' I helped him down from the table, which I then pushed back to its normal place. The grinding noise was thus explained. Hitler returned to bed and continued reading.

It was difficult to understand him. On the one hand he pandered even to the most unimportant things while on the other he was excessive and unfeeling. He might show the most fatherly concern for a female secretary who had stubbed her toe but be utterly ice-cold when issuing orders which sent thousands to their deaths. The 'privilege' of experiencing his concern was not necessarily an enjoyable affair. Thus all the tolerance he showed to me did not extend to my private habits of eating and drinking, for example. Here he was invasive. Frequently he tried to convince me how unhealthy it was to smoke. He considered that smoking was related to cancer and warned me persistently of its avoidable negative consequences. As his personal servant I had no option but to listen to this advice, which also included nutrition. Thus on 6 November 1941 Professor Hugo Blaschke, Hitler's dentist, who had just given the men of the bodyguard a dental check and was Hitler's guest at table at FHQ, was obliged to familiarise himself with Hitler's ideas of healthy eating. Hitler 'pursued the theme with great obstinacy', SA-Standartenführer Dr Werner Koeppen, Rosenberg's personal assistant recorded. He noted that according to Hitler 'the causes – or at least the probable effects' for most of the 'not yet fully understood diseases like cancer' were to be found 'in improper diet'.[1]

Those of us in Hitler's circle permanently knew his 'song', which he repeated often and vehemently, that the meat-free diet was the best recipe for health. The 'most disastrous stage in human development', he said, according to the notes I saw, was 'the day when man first ate cooked meat'. As usual, he surprised his listeners with his assertions. Blaschke was truly speechless when Hitler told him that Nature did not cut short to sixty or seventy years the lives of people living under natural conditions when their true lifespan should be 150 to 180 years. Measured by their phase of development, so Hitler taught, all animals whose nutrition was natural lived eight to ten times as long as their period of development to full maturity, whereas the flesh-eating and therefore unnatural human lived for only three to four times this period. If people lived sensibly, and by this he meant principally the abandonment of meat and animal fats in the diet, they would live to be 150 to 180 years of age, which had been the case in antiquity, as one could see from the sagas.[2]

I was not at table that evening and so I only have this second-hand. However, it was nothing new for me, for occasionally at table Hitler would launch into much longer monologues which covered ground already gone over several times before. Although Hitler would make a joke of it when reference was made to Tacitus's remark

---

1 Protocol at National Archive, Washington: EAP/05/44 report no. 54, p.2.
2 Ibid.

that his warriors 'even resorted to meat when the war situation was especially serious', he began to think about meat production for Germany once the Russian campaign began. At the end of October 1941 he considered increasing the sheep flock and removing the tax from mutton. As a result of the gain of territory in the east, he argued, it seemed a good idea to increase the sheep population from its present twelve million to 18.5 million. The aversion of the Germans to mutton would soon vanish once it was realised that it was tax free and amazingly cheap at only twenty pfennigs per pound.

Hitler would often speak on human nutrition, principally at times when he felt either in the best or worst of health. When delivering a discourse on human eating habits, he enjoyed watching the reactions of the 'carnivores', his ironical term for meat-eaters. Once, in the autumn of 1944 it looked for a while that Hitler might be thinking of abandoning vegetarianism under the influence of the ENT specialist Dr Erwin Giesing.[3] The physician, no 'yes-man', confronted Hitler with arguments which gave him cause to reflect. He told Hitler that human dentition, the stomach intestines and the digestive juices were 'constructed' to be a cross between the pure herbivorous and pure carnivorous, which meant that by nature the human could in no way be considered vegetarian. Hitler, whose inclination was always to follow Nature, listened attentively. Giesing stated that Nature, 'otherwise so practical, would quite certainly not produce digestive juices for animal albumin' in the human intestines if they were superfluous. This apparently seemed very plausible to Hitler, and he asked Giesing to provide him with the technical literature as soon as possible so that he could consider the question in depth. I am fairly sure that if Giesing had stayed longer with Hitler, or had come to him earlier, he would have convinced him to abandon some of his more unsound habits if he wanted to remain in control of his faculties over the longer term. Of course,

---

3 See Chapter 15 for further mention of Dr Giesing.

Giesing would never have converted Hitler to smoking or regular alcohol intake. Wine tasted to him 'so sour' that he thought it could be improved 'with a spoonful of sugar'. Beer, as he often informed us, he had liked very much when he was young, but now he found it 'too bitter'. As for nicotine, he agreed with Goethe that the odour of tobacco smoke was the vilest of all. Premature hardening of the veins and arteries of the heart and brain were considered by Hitler to be the consequence of smoking, and the cause of change to the heart muscle itself which could have fatal results. Tobacco was 'the brown man's revenge' on the white man for having 'brought him firewater' and thus damaging him. Anti-smoking zealots and Party members in high places lobbying for Hitler's affections proposed a ban on smoking in Party buildings and offices, but despite his basic opposition to smoking, which he considered to be as dangerous to health as eating meat, Hitler would not go so far as to impose the ban for fear of alienating or losing many of his supporters.

For the same reasons he had decided – according to his own statement – not to marry or admit publicly his relationship with Eva Braun. This latter was kept strictly secret. At the beginning I was of course also unaware that the young blonde who always sat at table near his left was his secret love.

Chapter 4

Eva Braun, the Question of Sexual Morality, and Equestrian Pursuits

ITLER HAD GOT TO know Eva Braun in 1932 at Heinrich Hoffmann's photographic studio and had soon become very friendly with her. Since she was employed by Hoffmann, who was always around Hitler taking photographs of him, at first I thought nothing of it. I did notice that Hitler treated this pretty girl in a special way but I put it down to her appearance. She had a very natural and pleasant manner, while her charm and graceful figure enchanted us all. When Hitler stayed on Obersalzberg, she was always invited.

Eva Braun came from a middle-class family. Her father was a highly thought-of Munich teacher who was in no way a 'Nazi'. The parents were invited only once as Hitler's guests at the Berghof. That Hitler and Eva Braun lived as man and wife at the Berghof I soon saw by chance. They had four rooms for their intimate life: two bedrooms and two bathrooms with connecting doors. I was responsible for the upkeep of these rooms. They had designed the plan for this private flat together. In the evenings when Hitler stayed at the Berghof he would usually be alone with Eva in his study before they retired. She would wear just a dressing gown or house-coat and drink sparkling wine while he would have tea. Once when I entered the study without knocking, Hitler and Eva Braun were embracing in the middle of the room. Blushing, I did an about-turn and disappeared. Public demonstrations of love and affection were not for public display for Hitler or Eva Braun, and so it was seen as very significant when in the presence of others he called her 'Schnaksi' one day, to which she addressed him ironically in return as 'Mein Führer'.

As in any marriage now and again there would be a falling out, and she would try to hide her tears from me, but I always knew when there had been a 'clash'. She kept to herself whatever had occurred. She never confided in Frau Mittelstrasser the housekeeper. She remained eternally the likeable and charming *gnädiges Fräulein*, as she was addressed officially, and there were never confidences or vulgarities on her part. As openly and sincerely as she confided to her diary what moved her, so little did she allow those unauthorised to share in it. Like all officers' women at FHQ – except at the end in Berlin – she was never allowed there. Hitler phoned her regularly. I often listened to these conversations, for after I asked him once if I should leave the room just after he had begun speaking he replied with a smirk: 'Don't concern yourself, I speak in a way that I do not mind anybody hearing what I say.' He liked to tease her, but he also listened when she talked, and he even made decisions based on her suggestions. One of these at least was certainly welcomed by women and girls during the war when Hitler wanted to close all the hairdressing parlours, and Eva convinced him against it. 'You expect to see a woman with a nice hair-do when you come home from the front', she told him in annoyance, 'and your soldiers?' Hitler raised his eyebrows and replied: 'Good, they can carry on making women beautiful then.'

If Hitler had time, and circumstances allowed, he would even visit Eva Braun from his HQs. Unlike him, she enjoyed sport and was a good skater, swimmer and skier. Hitler was not keen on skiing. When Eva went skiing with the film director and actor Luis Trenker, Hitler stepped in and told him to do his skiing elsewhere. Before I came to Hitler he had been once, as he often told people, a passable sportsman who had been active though generally alone. He used to ski, toboggan, swim and did regular exercises with the expander. For all I ever saw of these activities they belonged in the past, much to the regret of Eva Braun who would have liked nothing better than for him to accompany her in one of her favourite sports. He saw her when she skated or swam, but he was only ever there as a 'spectator'.

Hitler was utterly against being photographed in a bathing suit, as Ebert and Noske had been; in his opinion these two political leaders in the period immediately after the First World War had demeaned their authority after appearing in photographs in the August 1919 edition of the *Berliner Illustrierte* while paddling in the Haffkrug at Travemünde. On the other hand it did not worry him that Eva Braun was photographed in a bathing costume or skating dress.

At officials functions at the Berghof, in Munich or Berlin, at receptions and social occasions, Eva Braun would not appear. A Führer who was married or involved in a permanent liaison with a woman, Hitler used to say, would be rejected by a section of his female followers. Perhaps he was also thinking too that Eva Braun, if presented as his wife, might not be quite the kind of woman the world would expect a Frau Hitler to be. Eva probably sensed this and in her melancholy would look enviously at Frau Göring, who had mastered the role. If this was actually the case with Hitler I have no idea. He once said to her in my presence that he would 'make it all up to her later', what he had had to 'make her go through' over the years, but that may have been merely a phrase of consolation. 'When Germany no longer needs my leadership and I can hand over the reins of power to my successor with peace of mind', he promised her, 'then I will build myself a small house in Linz and live privately with you as my wife, concern myself with architecture and painting and write my memoirs.'

As to the fact that he gave Eva Braun the love of which he was capable there is no doubt. In 1936, as her diary proves, but of which

I had no knowledge at the time, she complained bitterly that Hitler only loved her when they were in bed together. Later, during the war, when he was at the front and in his HQs he had scarcely any time for her at all. The old love idyll of Obersalzberg was pushed into the background once the Russian campaign began. Yet Hitler did not forget his 'wife'. Every second day he would telephone her. When his senior adjutant or Bormann flew to Munich, he would give them letters for her. If he received presents, I would have to pass them on to her. He would write a couple of nice lines to enclose. If he flew to Munich or Berlin himself, obviously he would meet her. If the Berghof was used temporarily as his HQ, the old idyll would be rekindled, if under other conditions.

When total war was proclaimed and rationing of foodstuffs assumed ever tighter limits, the wives of men at the front worried that even on the short leave passes they were granted, there would not be sufficient varied fare to offer them. Hitler was strong on rationing and even accepted that it applied to himself. Eva Braun, who in her own way was more on the side of the womenfolk than the Party functionaries, requested Hitler to loosen the restrictions insofar as they affected wives whose men had leave from the front. Hitler gave in and promised that in such cases in future he would order the rationing regulations to be interpreted more liberally.

One day Eva gave vent to her heartfelt emotions by scolding Hitler for allowing soldiers of the Wehrmacht to act like village yokels in a discourteous, ignorant and boorish manner towards women. Apparently he had no idea what she was talking about since neither Bormann nor Himmler had reported any such incidents. He promised 'to introduce remedies' at once.

As the war neared its end and the Führer-HQ was transferred to Berlin, Eva came to Hitler in the Reich Chancellery bunker. At the beginning of February 1945 she went down to Munich to sort out her personal affairs. Hitler asked her to look after my wife and children whom I wanted to evacuate to the Berchtesgaden area because room

was need at the Reich Chancellery to create the HQ. He asked me
if during her temporary stay in Munich my wife had somewhere to
stay with the children. If she did not, she and the children could use
his flat there. When the group for the trip – Eva and Gretl Braun,
my wife and children – were making their way to the courier-train
for Munich, the Russians were well inside Reich territory, and in
the West the Allies were crossing the border. Our goodbyes were
correspondingly emotional.

My wife and I did not want to envisage the end and closed our
eyes in optimism, soothed by our children's chatter about 'dear
Uncle Führer' as they called Hitler. Eva, who impressed me as a
fine woman, did all she could to keep up our morale. On the journey
she asked my wife: 'Will you be returning to Berlin?' When told that
we no longer had a flat there, Eva Braun assured my wife calmly
and firmly: 'Whatever happens I am returning to Berlin. If the Boss
(she never called him Adolf or 'the Führer') does not send for me
within four weeks, I will go back to him on my own initiative. I am
standing by him.' She kept her promise and came back even though
she knew – or at least suspected – that it would mean the end of her
life. She was then thirty-three years of age, a beautiful, mature but
rather afflicted woman. The years with Hitler had left their mark.

How skilfully Hitler and Eva Braun hid their relationship from
outsiders 'at court' who kept their eyes and ears open is shown in the
replies of Hugo Blaschke on 19 November 1947 under interrogation
by Dr Robert M.W. Kempner at Nuremberg.[1] Blaschke was Hitler's
dentist from the end of 1933 until 20 April 1945, and Eva Braun was
also his patient, but he had hardly any information to give Kempner
about the relationship between the two of them. The fragments of
the interrogation, repeated below with Dr Kempner's permission,
are a good example of how Hitler and Eva concealed everything
from the close circle over the years:

---

1 Robert M.W. Kempner, *Das Dritte Reich im Kreuzverhör*, Munich and Esslingen
1969, pp.55ff.

Dr Kempner (K): Was Eva your patient?

Dr Blaschke (B): Yes.

K: Was she a good-looking person?

B: Yes.

K: What was funny about this person?

B: She was not intelligent. She liked to watch two films each day. If she could have, she would have watched four films each day. The funny thing is that I do not believe a man, despite the greatest self-control, can hide it if he really fancies a woman, although Hitler never showed it, like Göring. Over all the years I never saw anything to make me think he loved her. That is something a man would notice.

K: I don't know about that.

B: One is bound to notice, a gesture or something.

K: But you knew the other half did?

B: I didn't see. I didn't like her personally. After treating her for two months I transferred her to my assistant. I always had one so that someone would be in the picture and could treat the patient if I didn't have time.

K: Which of the women came to your practice?

B: Gretl Braun.

K: The future Frau Fegelein?

B: Yes. And then another friend, Herta Schneider. She was always up there when Eva was on the Berg.

K: Did Hitler watch when you treated Eva?

B: No.

K: You saw them together?

B: Eva sat at Hitler's left with Bormann on her left.

K: Eva was brunette?

B: A bit of peroxide, she wasn't pure blonde.

K: Dyed?

B: Blond. Given a bit of help. Made more blonde.

K: They didn't have children, or did they?

B: I didn't hear anything. She didn't have what one would call sex appeal. She dressed well. When I spent some weeks up there she never wore the same outfit twice. She was only about at midday and in the evenings. Often when tea was served in the Berghaus she would go down with them.

K: You say that nobody noticed that he loved her. But on the other hand, if one sits constantly with so prominent a personality, between Hitler and Bormann, one has to accept that there was something special?

B: She had the position, but the question for me is why. Over the fourteen years I sat well away from them and sometimes near them.

K: You never saw a tender glance?

B: If one grew up in Berlin's Westend, one knows it. Perhaps I have a feel for it too, observing people.

K: But there was never anything that struck you?

B: No.

K: From other circumstances one could infer it?

B: If I like a woman I hold her hand.

K: That would not be harmless?

B: No.

K: He never took hold of her in the presence of a third party?

B: No, he just kissed her hand. I found it funny the way he used to kiss the hand of all the married ladies. One of his secretaries got married, and afterwards he would also kiss her hand. He didn't before. I never kissed the hand of Eva Braun or any other lady. It means nothing to me. That was perhaps the reason there was such a difference between us.

For those of us who knew Hitler's relationship with Eva Braun from personal observation, the watchword until 29 April 1945 was 'see nothing, hear nothing, say nothing'. Thus it was not generally known until after the war that Hitler had had a long-term love relationship with Eva Braun. Whenever people came who did not belong within the closest circle Eva kept to her rooms. She made up for it by inviting female friends – Frau Speer, the wife of Hitler's travelling physician Karl Brandt or Frau Hoffmann, and got what she could out of her situation. Frequently her sister Gretl helped her to pass the time. Ilse Braun, her eldest sister, a very intelligent journalist, was friendly with a Jewish doctor and kept well away from the circle in which Eva found herself. Gretl, the middle one, we saw often, especially after she married Hermann Fegelein, Himmler's SS liaison officer to the Führer. Fegelein, a former horseman, advanced quickly as a result of this marriage. The highly decorated leader of a frontline SS cavalry division, he was quickly made SS-general and enjoyed a lot of grace and favour until shot by firing squad shortly before the capitulation. He felt very good and well protected in the circle around Hitler, to whom he was attracted as a moth to the light. With charm and presents he inveigled himself into everybody's good books and gave the impression of having a particular standing with Hitler which was not the case, for Hitler – a kind of technical brother-in-law – treated him formally and kept him emphatically at arm's length. As with everybody else Hitler called him by his surname while Fegelein would address Hitler as 'Mein Führer'. He used the familiar pronoun when conversing with Eva Braun, of course, and she always called him 'Hermann' which he considered a distinction. While he did not actually refer to it directly, he would attempt to imply that it was significant with regard to his relationship with Hitler. Scarcely anybody wanted anything to do with 'the Führer's brother-in-law', who came to regard his duties as a paid pastime and too often let it be known that he thought himself 'too good for the job'. He was not 'too good' for the post he occupied; on the contrary he was not the man for it, and he had to thank his relationship by marriage to Eva Braun for his position and the prestige.

How Eva Braun's conservative parents, who were initially opposed to the liaison between Adolf Hitler and their daughter

Eva, ever came to accept the SS son-in-law for daughter Gretl was something none of us ever worked out. I did know, however, that they eventually came to terms with Eva's decision to lead her own life and 'fit in' with Hitler according to her own ideas.

Outsiders – not infrequently guests – would ask me how Hitler stood on the question of 'women'. My answer that in this regard he shared the joyful weakness of all normal men satisfied most enquirers. Hitler was not blind to the attractions of the other sex. He loved pretty and intelligent women. He treated ladies with chivalry and gallantry. Scarcely anyone could ward off his likeability and the charm he radiated. In dresscoat and tails, or on special occasions such the Bayreuth Festival when he appeared in a white smoking jacket or white uniform, many of the women present would 'catch fire' so to speak, even though they might be being escorted by their husbands. Often I would be requested to make the Führer discreetly aware of a signal or even pass a declaration of interest. When Hitler was in the right mood he could fascinate women. Ladies from the arts, particularly actresses, would on occasion become very familiar with him, which caused him a certain difficulty, for I had the impression that he did not always find it so easy to reject all this worship and remain faithful to Eva.

Once Hitler found a love letter with a rose in his bed. I never discovered how the adoring female involved managed this. In 1932 during one of his electioneering tours across the Reich he had an experience in this connection which he would retell. After delivering a speech and returning to his hotel, a lady appeared with the intention of seeing him alone in his room. She was dressed in an expensive fur. His security people considered that the lady represented a risk for which reason they would not allow her to enter. Suddenly she opened the fur and screamed: 'Hitler tried to rape me!' Her dress under the fur was ripped. This was a plot, as was soon established, but if it had occurred in his room when they were alone Hitler would have been compromised and placed in an impossible position. Subsequently his security men had orders never to allow unknown women access, but even after 1933 they would occasionally succeed in evading the tight security guard. In June 1936 two women were arrested in the Reich Chancellery garden. Nobody found out how they got in.

Once I asked Hitler why he did not get married. He gave me a lecture on the destructive influence of women on great men and pointed out that, insofar as this question touched on the propaganda angle, he was anxious to appear to be the statesman who dedicated all his strength to the German people. To Otto Wagener, a former general staff officer and SA chief of staff from 1929 to 1932, who as leader of the NSDAP Political Economy Department was always close to Hitler's person, Hitler had explained:[2]

If I should be called upon to lead Germany out of despair, if I should succeed in becoming the hero of the German people, then the people should not be burdened with a son of mine. You see, where a great personality has emerged from nowhere and rises to magnificent heights, whether in the arts, science or as a statesman, the son has never been anything near what the father was. The children either slip back or fade into anonymity. Where is the son of Goethe, of Schiller, of Beethoven? What would Siegfried Wagner have become if, apart from being his father's son and inheriting Bayreuth, he had not had his mother Cosima as well as his equally significant life's companion Winifred with him? Or take Kant, or Napoleon. A son of mine would only be a burden and accordingly an unhappy person or a danger.

Hitler did not mention to Otto Wagener that by 'having a son' in this case he meant 'in wedlock', since he had already admitted to others beforehand his belief that he had a son, born in 1918 as the result of a relationship Hitler had had with a French girl as a

2 H.A. Turner jnr, *Hitler Aus Nächster Nähe: Aufzeichnungen Eines Vertrauten 1929–1932*, Frankfurt/Main, Berlin and Vienna 1978, p.99.

soldier in 1916–17 in northern France and Belgium, about which more later.

In any case, Eva Braun, who had had a happy family life in the parental home, as she liked to remember, had to give up any hope of bearing Hitler's son. Her two sisters Ilse and Gretl were also barren,[*] and so Hitler was simply 'Uncle Führer' for my children, and those of Goebbels, Bormann, Himmler and others in the environment.

The presence of Eva Braun and other women on Obersalzberg resulted in a quite different lifestyle there than at the Reich Chancellery in Berlin. Before I came to Hitler, he had his half-sister Angela as housekeeper for him on the Berg. She had helped Göring acquire a piece of land nearby, and through this had lost the trust of her half-brother who would not tolerate machinations of this kind. Within twenty-four hours, as Bormann informed me with glee, she had had to leave the Berg.

In March 1938, when German forces marched into Austria, Hitler met his full sister Paula in Vienna. I was present. He received her in the Hotel Imperial. At that time forty-four years old, she had not seen her brother for years, and was visibly impressed. Hitler had changed outwardly very much in the meantime. The meeting was heartfelt, the sister looking more or less overwhelmed. Deeply moved she shook Hitler's hand. He was visibly pleased to be able to meet her in Vienna as head of state of the German Reich. They were alone for about half an hour in Hitler's hotel room. What they spoke about I do not know. I had tea served to them and noticed that they were in animated conversation. During their farewell, Hitler's sister, a cultivated and very motherly figure, was given about 100 RM in an envelope. She was not well off: her gestures could not be interpreted in any other way, although by her attire she was not on Vienna welfare benefits. I never saw her again. When the end was approaching in 1945, Hitler gave an SD man the job of getting a few

---

[*] Unknown to Linge, Gretl Fegelein gave birth to a daughter in May 1945. (TN)

hundred RM to Paula by roundabout means (if I am not mistaken it was 400 RM).*

In Munich, where we did not stay very often, Anny Winter ran Hitler's seven-room flat at Prinz-Regenten-Strasse 16. As with a number of other people, she found herself in Hitler's circle without any prior intent on her part. As Hitler needed an administrator and housekeeper for the flat, one day he asked publisher Max Amann, his sergeant from the First World War and owner of the Franz-Eher Verlag which published *Mein Kampf*, if he knew a suitable female person for the job. Amann promised to 'ask around' and one day produced the wife of one of his book packers. This was Anny Winter. As soon as we arrived together at Hitler's flat she literally took him by the hand and led him into the study, there to give him all 'the latest news', that is, gossip about artistes, businessmen, Party members and especially the housewives of Munich's corner-shops. Anny Winter knew 'everything', more or less, and Hitler, the erstwhile frequenter of Vienna coffee houses, enjoyed listening. Julius Schaub was on the same wavelength as Anny Winter and filled in the few gaps in her knowledge.

Although Hitler kept mostly to his daily work schedule at the Berghof, amongst the guests at least the days were ones of relaxed sociability. Prewar the Berghof resembled a holiday hotel in glorious surroundings. While Hitler worked during the mornings, the guests amused themselves, sunbathing in deckchairs, playing table-tennis, chatting on the terrace or rambling in the magnificent mountains. Eva Braun, keen on photography and filming, would always be involved in one way or another.

---

* Christa Schroeder, *He Was My Chief: The Memoirs of Hitler's Secretary*, London 2009, p.41. Hitler supported his sister with a monthly allowance of 250 Austrian schillings, and from 1938 to 1945 with 500 RM monthly. On 14 April 1945 she was brought by the SS to Berchtesgaden under the name 'Paula Wolf' where on Hitler's instructions she received from SS Obergruppenführer Julius Schaub the sum of 100,000 RM (BayHSTA, Munich, 5 May 1951). (TN)

The occasional sporting events in Munich which we attended as spectators were a special diversion from the daily monotony. The only leading Nazi who was also an active top-rank sportsman was Reinhard Heydrich. He rode, fenced, flew and sailed yachts, and was master of them all. As a sportsman he always caught the eye, was always fair and gladly received. As soon as he donned his fencing apparel he ceased to be Gestapo chief and was only a sportsman. He did what Göring, Goebbels, Rosenberg and Ley unctuously recommended everybody should do. Hitler was interested in sport although he did not participate himself. He liked to watch ice hockey, football and boxing. That Max Schmeling was amongst his welcome guests was no coincidence.

I noticed that Hitler was very nervous about the possibility of Germans losing in international competitions. In the stadium he would fidget, move his head nervously and knead his hands. In this respect he resembled Mussolini, though the latter partook of sport and enjoyed horse-riding, which Hitler found 'a bit funny'. He was not himself a lover of horses because their brains were too small which accounted for their stupidity. Moreover as warlord and strategist he was committed single-mindedly to the need for technological advances, and he did not think there was much more that could be achieved with the horse in warfare. He thought it had probably served its purpose as 'the motor in history'. All this did not prevent his admiring paintings of horses, however, and he had two larger-than-life illustrations commissioned from Josef Thorak for the New Reich Chancellery. The natural beauty, the nobility, the harmony of movement and the power of the horse as an artistic subject fascinated Hitler the painter. Moreover he saw in it impressive justification of the success of man's guiding hand in horse-breeding. He was very reluctant to tolerate artistic representations of himself as a knight on a horse. 'Myself on a horse', he said once, 'impossible, unimaginable.'

Perhaps it was not coincidence that with the exception of Heydrich none of the National Socialist exponents was a 'known' horseman. Göring also rode a bit, but he did it secretly on the Schorfheide seen only by his stable staff dressed in fantasy uniforms designed by himself. Before the war Göring weighed more than 100 kilogrammes, and Hitler did not approve of Göring using an animal of world renown for his gallops over the heath. This was the big grey Wotan, which had won the coveted Mussolini Cup at the Concorso Ippico in Rome in 1933 against strong competition from the Poles, Italians and the Spanish. Göring had acquired the horse 'in a roundabout way': he was thinking of 'slimming down' and reckoned that horse-riding was a good way to achieve his goal. In vain. Göring never lost an ounce, and that was long before the war during which he would typically weigh in at anything up to 122 kilogrammes. Göring never took offence at Hitler's jokes about the 'surging take-offs' and 'flights at low altitude' by his 'equestrian air marshal' since he perceived in them a degree of the Führer's recognition and respect.

Hitler generally knew what the people in his close circle did privately, but he never asked anybody to spy and keep him updated. He would talk to this or that person and ask conversationally what he did when not on duty, but he was opposed to gossip and would put a stop to any attempt to pass him information about third parties. Personal liaisons only interested him if they concerned himself directly or were intruding into the field of politics, as was the case with Goebbels on one occasion. Only once do I recall that he actually sought my 'advice' in this respect. In 1942, a man of his immediate circle seen relatively often in his presence had married a former prostitute, a fact of which Hitler was unaware. The wife had been married previously to a member of the SS bodyguard who had fallen on the Eastern Front. As the first marriage had been celebrated after she gave up her career as a call girl, she had managed to keep this activity hidden. The second marriage now brought her into the Führer's close circle. Kaltenbrunner heard the rumours and confirmed that they were true. 'What would happen if the Führer found out?' we asked ourselves. Nobody – neither Himmler nor Kaltenbrunner nor Bormann nor Schaub – wanted to tell him, and when in Hitler's presence the conversation got round to the 'happy young couple' we tended to study our fingernails. Obviously this could not go on. Himmler and Kaltenbrunner ganged up on Bormann to inform Hitler. Scarcely had he spilled the beans than Hitler sent for me and asked: 'Tell me, do you know Frau X?[3] She has been your neighbour for some time. What do you think of her?' Since I had discovered that when her husband was away she kept other men company in bed, I was able to answer with a clear conscience: 'For me, mein Führer, she is a whore!' He looked at me calmly and asked how I knew. After telling him what I had observed and been told, he reflected: 'Children, children, why didn't you tell me before? We really cannot tolerate that sort of thing here.' The result of our conversation was his instruction that the marriage must be annulled, which was done. The divorced husband remained with the lady, however, which Hitler was prepared to overlook. After the war I saw the couple again. After the SS-Führer's release from internment, they remarried.

'What people do in their beds', Hitler used to say, 'does not interest me so long as relationships do not prejudice the State and its leadership.' And he kept to that.

Rumours began to circulate about the wife of one of his adjutants. It was said that she had previously led a loose life, something that could eventually compromise her husband's position with the Führer. How Hitler found out about this I have no idea. Possibly from Bormann. Hitler told me that he did not want to act on gossip and summoned the wife to meet him. It was my job to drive her up

---

3 Christa Schroeder, *He Was My Chief: The Memoirs of Hitler's Secretary*, London 2009, p.196. According to Christa Schroeder this was the wife of Hitler's driver and vehicle park commandant SS Sturmbannführer Kempka.

from the railway station. Charming and very pleasant, she chattered to me throughout the drive. Hitler received her in a friendly, calm manner. As I knew him very well by now, I suspected how the conversation would go after seeing the sort of look he gave this beautiful and fascinating woman as she went in. When the door re-opened after a good long time and Hitler took his leave of her with a smirk I knew that I had judged it aright. The marriage was consolidated and the adjutant retained his post.

We who had been 'worried' had now to endure a lecture from Hitler which cut to the quick. The lady (he did not use the word 'wife') was not only strikingly pretty but also extremely intelligent and clever, and he praised her 'disarming candidness'.[4] 'What a bunch of sanctimonious moral apostles you all are', he said sarcastically, and treated us like naughty schoolboys. Afterwards he took me aside, gave me a stare and then asked in roughly these words: 'Linge, why did you remove your boots when you crept past my bedroom in the early hours? Were you trying not to wake me, or was I not supposed to know how keen you are on *night walks?*' His emphasis on 'night walks' was more than enough to get his meaning over. When I attempted to explain that my intention had been to avoid disturbing his sleep, I could see from his expression what he thought. He knew that I was not being entirely honest.

---

4 Christa Schroeder, *He Was My Chief: The Memoirs of Hitler's Secretary*, London 2009, p.196. According to Christa Schroeder this was the wife of Korvettenkapitän Alwin-Broder Albrecht, Hitler's personal adjutant.

Chapter 5

The Berghof

O N THE BERGHOF BEFORE the war Hitler liked to work into the early hours, or talk amongst his intimate circle, and would be woken 'unofficially' at ten o'clock unless urgent political business forced him to rise earlier. I would sort the morning papers, and the first foreign despatches which would have been brought from the Reich Chancellery during the night, and put them on a chair outside his bedroom. At eleven o'clock I would waken him 'officially' with the words: 'Good morning, mein Führer, it is eleven o'clock. The newspapers and despatches are at your door.' He would rise, fetch the post and read it in bed. Sometimes he would open the door in nightshirt and slippers while I was laying the material on the chair. Initially this kind of encounter was rather embarrassing for me and I would stammer my apologies, but Hitler, always unforced and natural, would merely say: 'It's nothing. Just leave them.'

He then read the newspapers and despatches in bed, near which there would be a tea-trolley with books, newspapers, his spectacles and a box with coloured pencils. What he might have been reading – or what interested him especially – could never be determined, for he never underlined nor marked anything, not even in books. After the morning reading session he would shave, remove his white nightshirt, lay it on the bed, bath, take the clothing ready on the clothes-stand and dress. Forty minutes after waking he would take breakfast in the library near the bedroom. Breakfast was frugal – only tea or milk, biscuits or sliced bread and an apple. During breakfast he read the menu card for lunch.

Two vegetarian courses, both including the obligatory apple, were provided for him to choose from. If strangers came to lunch, Hitler's food was arranged in such a way that the absence of meat was not obvious at first glance. After breakfast Hitler would greet his adjutants and myself and proceed with us to the rooms set aside for conferences with foreign visitors and businessmen. From about 1936 one of my duties was to ensure that his reading spectacles were always within reach when he needed them. He wore them as necessary in private but would never appear in public wearing them. 'The Führer', he explained to me, 'does not wear glasses.' Nevertheless when in a small circle he would toy with them in his hands which often resulted in their being broken when he got tense. I had to carry a reserve with me everywhere so that he would never be without reading glasses when he needed them. I also had to make sure that atlases, a magnifying glass, compasses, writing materials and red, green and blue coloured pencils were always to hand. Psychologists may draw conclusions from something Hitler explained to me in a moment of humour: 'The red pencils I use to make notes about an enemy. The green ones when it concerns somebody towards whom I am well disposed. The blue ones when I feel it is advisable to be cautious.'

Hitler was notorious for sleeping in, and it might be that the midday meal, attended by an average of ten to twelve guests, would not be served until 1430, by which time many guests would have satisfied their appetites by eating elsewhere. Apart from Goebbels, his constant lunch guest before the war, and the close staff, Hess, Göring, Reich ministers and Party leaders would often dine at the Berghof. Hitler would usually greet his guests in the lounge before going into the dining room. He would escort one or other of the ladies, and the guests would take their pre-arranged seats. Eva Braun always sat at his left. The table talks in the prewar period were very lively and much influenced by the feminine presence. Most of all he enjoyed their weaknesses, of which he would occasionally provide illustrations. In the event of disputes which occasionally separated the ladies into different camps, he would be called up as the 'supreme judge', a role he discharged with humour. Once the ladies argued about the best way to prepare Bavarian meatballs. Hitler, asked for his judgement, sent them all into the kitchen to prove their respective arguments. A competition ensued. When the meatballs were brought in the men had to deliver their opinions. The orderly was a little unnerved by the unusual scene and allowed his meatballs to roll off his plate and across the table. He straightened up like a pillar of salt immediately, expecting a rocket from Hitler, but none was forthcoming. Instead, Hitler saved the situation by spearing a couple of the meatballs, the guests following his example.

At the midday meal, there would usually be soup, a main course and dessert, with drinks served to order. Hitler's meals were prepared lukewarm after an operation on his vocal chords made his voice sensitive. The conversation at table would be unforced and lively. After the meal there would be talks with Hess, Göring and other politicians or military men, who would generally stay to take tea with Hitler. His diet consisted principally of potatoes and vegetables, a stew without meat, and fruit. Normally there was no obligation on guests to accept limits to what they ate. Hitler once poked fun at Göring at a lunch just before the invasion of Norway in April 1940, when Admiral Raeder and the chief of the *Seekriegsleitung* were guests. Göring had a meat course with potatoes and asparagus, and Hitler looked at Göring's plate and remarked: 'People say that the pig eats potatoes, but nobody would dare say that the pig eats asparagus.' Göring joined in the general laughter.

Hitler would occasionally have beer with his meal, and wine on official occasions when a toast was due to be made. He was a strict vegetarian and non-smoker but was not opposed to alcohol. He gave up beer in 1943 when he began to put on fat around the hips and midriff. It did not disturb him to see others drinking, but he found drunkenness repulsive. After a reception for artistes an adjutant drank 'over the limit' and kissed the hand of every lady as she departed, causing Hitler to fear that the man might next commit an impropriety. Later in the adjutant's presence he imitated the scene to others. What he meant was unmistakable and showed the depth of his repressed anger.

After the midday meal Hitler liked to go to the lower tea-house. An adjutant or a minister summoned for a conference would accompany him, the ladies going on ahead. There was always a free and easy atmosphere in the tea-house. Hitler would sit by the fireplace fighting off sleep – because of his long night vigils – while the guests chatted amongst themselves.

At dinner, taken before Hitler attacked his real workload, generally only a few guests would be present. It would begin around eight in the evening, and at its conclusion Hitler would choose from a list the film to be shown later in the Large Hall. There would be a wide selection of recent releases as well as oldies. He would rise first, kiss the hand of his female neighbours and the lady seated opposite him and then proceed to the lounge. There all would converse like a family circle and pass the time with games while Hitler had brief talks in the Great Hall with people from his close staff. Afterwards he would invite his guests to the film show. There was no church-like silence as in public cinemas. The films were shown accompanied by loud comments and often ribald laughter. Everybody could attend these presentations. The day would conclude at the hearth, alcoholic drinks would be served and Eva Braun would sometimes prepare a snack. In the case of disputes I would have to fetch the lexicons or historical works at which Hitler, who had a fantastic memory, would usually indicate which volume was to be consulted, and also the page number. Since he never dictated the subjects for discussion, it would not have been possible for him to cram up beforehand in order to impress with his knowledge. These discussions might be interrupted for despatches and important reports in the evening papers, or for conferences with colleagues or military men, which would delay his timetable to such an extent that he would have to sit up through the early hours working in the library.

To break the monotony of daily life at the Berghof there would be visits to concerts, theatres, variety shows and other artistic presentations. Before 1939 Hitler liked to picnic near and far. I always accompanied him on these excursions and knew the Hitler we preferred: jovial, comradely and unproblematic. When a good spot was found the column of vehicles would halt. Rugs would be laid out in shady woods or on pastureland, beer and wine served. People ate and drank what they fancied, told anecdotes and jokes (in good taste), recounted experiences and made future plans. Hitler would sit or stretch out in our midst on a blanket and join in but he would not take drink or smoke. On the first of these trips when I went along it surprised me how he completely shed being 'the Führer', something which I had considered literally impossible. He even joined us when, full of beer and wine, we answered the call of nature. True he had only had Fachinger mineral water or tea or coffee, but the effect was the same as alcohol.

In Russian captivity under interrogation I was often asked if I had seen Hitler's genitals, and if so had they been normal. I had no idea why the Russians wanted to know this, but I told them what I knew. Naturally I had not seen Hitler fully naked even once. When the Russians interrogators alleged that Hitler 'had only had one ball' I had to laugh, and for doing so they gave me a whipping. However odd this interest of theirs might seem it was tied to the conviction of the Russians that I must have had sex with Eva Braun myself because they assumed 'Hitler had not been able to'. That he 'had been able to' I was sufficiently convinced. My observations led me to believe that the sexual relationship between Hitler and Eva Braun had been especially active on occasion. I do not know which of the two was the more active. Eva Braun could be very sexy in the modern terminology and so I suppose was Hitler.

Chapter 6

The Reich Chancellery, Bayreuth, the Aristocracy and Protocol

ITLER'S RECEPTIONS IN BERLIN before the war were held in the former Bismarck Palace within the Old Reich Chancellery in the Wilhelm-Strasse. The old Congress Hall was in need of renovation and could no longer be used. Representatives from industry, the arts, the Party, the Wehrmacht and the state were his guests. The first great reception in the new dining hall on Hitler's instruction brought together industrialists. Hitler did not want just a glamorous event – his primary aim was to win over this sceptical sector so important for his policies. Thus it was understandable that he took care of the preparations himself. The guests were not disappointed. Famous artistes, musicians, singers and La Scala Ballet, many of the personalities known only from conversations, radio broadcasts and press reports appeared. Erna Sack and a number of Wagnerian singers gave the evening special appeal.

Hitler welcomed his guests with a brief address in which he explained how this personal contact would be of advantage to both sides. It was interesting for me to see how the individual industrialists reacted. The initial reserve put on for show soon began to melt. A relaxed mood set in at the tables. Hitler's charm and attentiveness had quickly done the trick. He dedicated a few minutes personally to each of his guests, moving from table to table talking. One saw that many were surprised by Hitler's versatility and knowledge. Not a few had undoubtedly come simply to see the propagandist orator at close quarters, and when they left their host most had certainly changed their minds about him, taking home with them a fresh impression of Hitler.

Beforehand they had been outfoxed when he appealed to 'the fat wallets' of the captains of industry and mentioned that the artistes and performers had wanted to contribute their earnings for the night to the *Winterhelfswerk* relief fund. A donation list did the rounds. The 'heads of industry' signed their names and the amounts they would donate. Finally the document lay on Hitler's table. He perused it, took a pen and wrote in one million RM. Within a few seconds the news had gone round the hall. A million Reichmarks. The industrial magnates took a deep breath, and many asked for the list to be brought back to them to add one or two noughts to their original contribution. Hitler, who had gambled on the influence and vanity of the wives, had been proved right. After a quiet whisper to their husbands and encouraging gestures the industrialists had given in. Hitler had triumphed. A few million more Reichsmarks would flow into the coffers of the *Winterhilfswerk*. Once the guests had gone, Hitler slapped me on the shoulder and said: 'A total success, an excellent result. Everything turned out wonderfully.' Soon I had forgotten the secret doubts which he admitted to me not only before the event but also during the gala evening itself.

Later similar events followed this 'prototype' under Hitler's direction. Exclusive aristocratic circles, for which Hitler had little affection, a fact he only rarely made known, kept their distance at first, but Hitler found a way. Frau von Dirksen,[1] one of his faithful followers, offered herself as an intermediary. Before the seizure of power she had arranged access for him to the so-called 'Gentlemen's Club' around Franz von Papen. Even when Hitler was very busy, he

---

1 Born 8 May 1877.

always had time for Frau von Dirksen, who wrote to him frequently when she was on her travels so that he generally knew where she would be. Her personal contacts to the house of Hohenzollern did not worry him. When he heard that she was meeting with Hermine, wife of the former kaiser, he was unperturbed.

One day Frau von Dirksen introduced her niece to Hitler. Sigrid von Laffert was one of the most beautiful women I ever saw in Hitler's entourage and enchanted everybody. Hitler invited her to all festive occasions. Her unusual beauty and spirit lent Hitler's parties a special glamour, and generally she would be the centre of attention of all the guests. In order to secure her for his close circle, Hitler wanted her to marry the Foreign Ministry representative Hewel, but she was apparently only interested in Hitler. It was not unusual for me to hear him urging Hewel to make himself known as a suitor, but nothing came of it. Sigrid von Laffert, painted by Ferdinand Staeger at Hitler's request, eventually married a titled nobleman at the Germany embassy in Madrid.[2]

Although the Führer accepted the presence of certain aristocrats, they were never a 'component' of his 'court'. He remained highly suspicious of them. If they became the subject of conversation he would occasionally speak of 'my princes', but it was not hard to detect the irony in his remarks. If one of them rendered a service to the Party, which rarely happened, then things were different. Philipp von Hessen, nephew of the former kaiser and son-in-law of the last king of Italy, was a welcome guest until the summer of 1943 when he and his Italian wife disappeared into a concentration camp. Philipp had rendered Hitler diplomatic services particularly in Italy, and had been something approaching the Führer's 'royal courier'. After Mussolini was overthrown, he was 'dead' for Hitler.[*]

---

2 Reproduced in Werner Maser, *Adolf Hitler – Legende – Mythos – Wirklichkeit*, Munich 1971, p.401 (illustration 47). She married Graf Hans Welczek, an official at the Madrid embassy.

* Hitler believed Philipp von Hessen was complicit in Mussolini's downfall. He

Hitler considered it very important to gather around himself prominent members of the middle classes: artists, scientists, authors, industrialists and *Alte Kämpfer*. Before the war he had also invited leaders of youth organisations with their wives. He observed with satisfaction after one such evening: 'There are women here who would excite even in the so-called best society. An aristocracy is emerging from within the people on which we can build with confidence.' Hitler's faith in the artistic strata was based not least on the fact that hardly any of them had political ambitions, although many – Hans Albers, for example – had been Party members from early on. Often he would say that one must allow people 'almost every idiosyncrasy' but he would not forgive everything: criticism of National Socialism, of himself as Führer and his state – this had to be punished. With magnanimity he would overlook utterances and confessions that displeased him, such as criticisms of his own guests or those of the Fraternity of German Artists. There Hitler was treated as in the Reich Chancellery as the Führer and head of state, but the atmosphere in which Max Schmeling and Anny Ondra felt especially comfortable was more free and open.

After the war in artistes' memoirs I read occasional reports about such meetings in which the authors claimed that they were treated by Hitler on equal terms, they called him 'Herr Hitler' and quite often of course they had enlightened him about certain things. The fact is, however, that 'mein Führer' was literally fawned over by many of these people, and none of them met Hitler without a special show of respect. Max Schmeling, Anny Ondra, Gustav Knuth, Leni Riefenstahl, these and all the rest who were Hitler's guests enjoyed the invitations and thanked the Führer in a most obsequious manner,

---

was given favourable treatment and survived spells in Flossenbürg and Dachau to be freed by the Allies. Hitler was convinced that Philipp's wife, Princess Mafalda of Savoy, was working against the German war effort. She died in August 1944 as the result of injuries sustained during an Allied air raid on Buchenwald concentration camp. (TN)

thanked the man of whom he liked it to be said that he was one of them and did a lot for them.

Occasionally it would happen that upon visiting Hitler – via Bormann, Lammers, Meissner or one of the adjutants – invitees would attempt to glean from me immediately before entering advice as to how they could make 'the best impression on the Führer'. It was not always so-called nobodies who posed this question. Many 'Great Men of the Reich' asked it, but mostly added 'today'. They wanted to know 'how the Führer is disposed today' before the door into his presence was opened. How did I reply to first-time visitors? I usually told them 'to look the Führer straight in the eye' and unburden their hearts to him without preamble. That Hitler laid firm value on a firm handshake was something I kept to myself: for some reason I did not think it appropriate that it should be mentioned expressly.

One of the visitors who might have profited from such advice was Bernhard, prince of Lippe-Biesterfeld, who had married Crown Princess Juliana of The Netherlands in 1937. Although as a former Party member – and now Prince Bernhard of The Netherlands, as Hitler recounted with disdain – he had always maintained how closely he felt the tie to his 'Fatherland Germany'. Hitler realised when they took their leave of each other that he had been dealing with a 'windbag'. 'When I offered him my hand in parting', Hitler said, 'I held a lazy, limp leaf.' The 'reorientation of the prince's conscience and feelings' was 'treason to Volk and Fatherland'. If Hitler originally thought that, by the presence of the prince in Amsterdam and The Hague, he could build a bastion of the Reich there, that handshake alone had shown him that he was sadly mistaken.

Whoever was not received – and over the course of time that was very, very many – was advised to register in the guest book. Hitler had mostly no interest in who had registered an attendance, even though the book contained the name of foreign automobile manufacturers and German diplomats and delegations from all over the world. So far as I can establish, a study of these guest books, which from 1938 were stored at Braunau and Leonding where Hitler spent his childhood, has never been undertaken. They were certainly not without interest. After the annexation of Austria, Bormann told Hitler that a Jewish gentleman from the United States had offered to buy the Hitler house at Leonding with the intention of dismantling it and shipping it for rebuilding true to the original in the States; Hitler merely shook his head in disbelief. Bormann, who had acquired the house with Party funds and had it renovated, told Hitler of names and entries in the Leonding register which might be important eventually, especially since a good proportion of them were inserted by personalities of note. Aristocrats, entrepreneurs, scientists and artists had made entries – most with an effusive dedication. Although Hitler listened with interest, he let it drop.

Those not in the know may find it difficult to understand how the system of visitor-approval worked. If for example Lammers, Meissner or Bormann had informed an applicant for audience that the Führer would receive him, it might so happen that I would reject the person literally at Hitler's door because something was 'not in order'. If I saw that somebody had a cold, for example, I was not to allow him entry to the 'Boss'.

For my dealings with Hitler over the course of time I developed a certain way of doing things which enabled me to meet his expectations, tolerate his whims and not disturb his habits without too much expenditure of energy. Right at the beginning it seemed most important to me never to provide him with cause to distrust me. On the occasions when I did something that he would probably view as 'out of order' I would not wait until he found out, but admit it to him voluntarily at once. As he valued the courage to be honest, as he called it, such admissions would usually incur no real disciplinary action. As the war went on, particularly if he wanted to encourage a military man to be more honest in reporting his errors, occasionally he would make the observation: 'Even when he has really screwed up, I can never go to town on Linge because he always admits his errors as early as possible and thus takes the wind out of my sails.'

All the same, I cannot say that there was never any friction. Frequently I would receive a 'rocket' which appeared to me unjustified. When Hitler once inferred from my behaviour that I considered myself to have been unjustly treated, he told me: 'Linge, you are with me. Therefore, even when you are innocent I have to bawl you out. And I have to do it with sufficient vigour to ensure that you will take steps to pass it on to the culprits below you. I cannot always look for them myself.'

However unforced the relationship was with his close circle, he set clear limits to prevent attempts at familiarity. He used the familiar pronoun 'Du' between himself and Eva Braun, whom he called 'Schnaksi', only when they were alone, although he used 'Du' openly with the Wagner family at Bayreuth. Before I came to him in 1935, I was told that he used the familiar pronoun with the *Alte Kämpfer* Ernst Röhm and Hermann Esser amongst others. He had met the Wagner family for the first time in 1925 at Bayreuth, being introduced as a guest by the Bechstein piano family from Obersalzberg. He had gone there unwillingly, so he assured everybody, because Siegfried Wagner, the son of the composer, had been 'a little in the hand of the Jews'. It was less this alleged Jewish influence upon Siegfried Wagner than the consideration that his presence with them might cause them financial damage that gave him doubts, however. It seemed to him then, and I found that especially interesting, more important to keep the Wagner family above water than to liberate them from 'the hand of the Jews'. He had therefore travelled to Bayreuth with mixed feelings, but been 'converted' by the warmth and approval with which Lotte Wagner, for example, had received him. 'On the very first day', he said, 'she brought flowers to my hotel.' Over the next few days, in leather shorts, and often accompanied by artistes, Hitler drove up into the Fränkische Schweiz mountains or the Fichtelgebirge or wandered through the town like a tourist studying the architecture closely. Although it had not been so long since his world-famous putsch attempt of 8 and 9 November 1923, and the subsequent Hitler–Ludendorff trial, Hitler had nevertheless remained quite 'unknown' so that he was mostly unmolested. In the evenings, he went on, he had worn a dress coat and tails, and after the performances used to go to the 'Eule' guesthouse where he met the artistes appearing at the Festival – who 'naturally knew him'.

From 1935 as Hitler's escort I had myself automatically been a guest at the Bayreuth Festivals. For the first two years I had private lodgings and then Hitler arranged for me to stay at Villa Wahnfried, where there was a guesthouse at his disposal. He operated this as host and reserved a room for me. In Hitler's entourage would be mainly the Reich press chief Dr Dietrich, Speer, Martin Bormann, Dr Theo Morell and Karl Brandt, Hitler's adjutants, invited military men and others of his permanent circle. They would follow us in the convoy from the Berghof. On the way Hitler would either wear uniform, or civilian attire with a droopy, wide-brimmed hat which made him look like a Bavarian folk poet. At Bayreuth, Hitler belonged to the Wagner family, and many onlookers looking in from behind the hedges suspected that Hitler's dealings with Winifred Wagner concealed a secret love affair. Whoever saw the pair of them walking hand in hand or arm in arm in the Villa Wahnfried parkland might have taken them for a married couple, and it certainly looked that way. Bayreuth Week was always a period of convalescence for ourselves and Hitler, from which he would long draw the benefit. Repeatedly he would return the conversation to events at the Festival and become re-animated.

Before the war Goebbels was Hitler's lunch guest almost daily. Hitler liked to give him full rein at table. Spirited and sarcastic, Goebbels enlivened the table conversation with amusing episodes. He liked to repeat criticism and jokes currently circulating about himself within the population. Frequently he would poke fun at himself. Whoever was the butt of jokes and anecdotes, he explained, was popular amongst the people, and also loved. The extent to which he was prepared to go is illustrated by the following:

> Two flies, so went a joke current in Berlin at the time, sat in one corner of Goebbels' mouth. They decided to have a bet. Whichever fly arrived first in the other corner of his mouth would win. One flew to the back of Goebbels' head and claimed he had won. When the loser asked for an explanation, the winner replied: 'You forgot that he talks out of the back of his head.'

After the delighted roar of laughter which followed the punch line, Hitler observed that he was considering renaming the Reich Chancellery 'the Hotel of the Jovial Reich Chancellor'.

However much he may have enjoyed irony aimed at major figures who could defend themselves, he would react with disapproval towards anybody being 'victimised' who had no means of defence. Thus he criticised the Prussian king Friedrich Wilhelm I for maltreating Jakob Paul Grundling, president of the Berlin Academy of Sciences, by locking him in a bear cage with a wine barrel for the amusement of his guests and making him wear clown's costume. Although to his close circle Hitler mocked particular callings such as teachers and priests, contrary to Friedrich Wilhelm I he did not ridicule the academic world even if in general he despised the intelligentsia. Until the outbreak of war Hitler laughed and joked often. In 1940 during the French campaign he lost the ability relatively suddenly. Previously he had been very restrained only before strangers.

The German–Jewish journalist Konrad Heiden, born at Frankfurt/Main, who was especially well-known after 1933 for his books about Hitler and National Socialism,[3] portrayed Hitler – falsely in one respect – in one of his books, which Hitler read. For

---

3 Principally Konrad Heiden, *Geschichte des National Sozialismus*, Hamburg 1932; *Geburt des Dritten Reiches*, 2nd edn Zurich 1934; *Adolf Hitler*, vol. II, Zurich 1936.

Heiden, Hitler was an unrefined artisan who, rather than play a violin, would chop it up for its wood to grill a cutlet. In fact, Hitler not only read enormously but also went often to the theatre or the opera, attended art exhibitions and studied architecture every free moment he had with the aim of appearing sure-footed and worldly at every opportunity. Not in vain in 1932 had he taken instruction in stage presentations from the popular operatic tenor Paul Devrient.

On 29 September 1938 Hitler committed a gaffe during the Munich Conference by sitting down before his guests Mussolini, Daladier and Chamberlain had taken their seats, but this lack of respect might equally well have been a deliberate demonstration of his power. Perhaps he was too excited and forgot protocol, for before official receptions he was always a little nervous. Then he would concern himself with the smallest details. The floral arrangement, the cutlery at table and suchlike were controlled by him. The architect in him would then come to the forefront. Once he had regained his peace of mind he would be the master of every situation.

Hitler's clothing was usually a poor fit. This was for two reasons. He said he did not need an expensive wardrobe and he did not like clothing that restricted his movements. 'I feel as though I am hanging up when the shirt collar and jacket are made the way it suits the creators of fashion,' he explained once. Eva Braun made various attempts to change this. 'If only the Führer could be a snappy dresser like Count Ciano', she told me once and recommended that I urge the Boss 'not to look like the eternal sentry'. Neither of us was successful. Hitler would not wear what was fashionable, but only what he felt comfortable in. Once when we tried to give his service cap a more elegant shape, he protested brusquely and demanded: 'Return my hat as it was. It is I who have to wear it, not you.' On his simple brown uniform he wore the gold Party badge and only two decorations from the First World War – the Iron Cross First Class and the Wound Badge in black. His civilian attire was made to a cut, which suited him. Even if the impression disappointed, Hitler was nevertheless vain and always made an effort, at least in evening dress, to make a good impression.

Early on I had to go through a procedure based on one of his sporting whims. He always dressed himself, and he did this to a stopwatch, my presence being as a kind of referee. At his command *Los!* I set the watch going and the dressing race began. The quicker he finished the better his temper. Standing before the mirror, eyes closed, Hitler required my help only for the bow-tie, which also had to be done in record time. He counted the seconds, and as soon as I said 'finished' he would open his eyes and check in the mirror how the bow-tie looked. The hairdresser and tailor were also required to work at the double. Hitler's characteristic lock of hair, which always lay across his forehead – and his moustache – always attracted a lot of friendly amusement amongst the population. He knew this and took great pride in both. Whether he was copying Napoleon's hairstyle I have no idea. Even as a schoolboy he parted his hair on the right for a while. His moustache was often a clue to his mood. If he was sucking it, this was always a warning for us.

My work was the cause of a lot of annoyance for me. Apart from his wardrobe I would often have to pack fifteen to twenty trunks when we travelled. These contained his books, office materials, medications, and so on. His tie would often cause him great aggravation. The one he wanted would often not be found. Then he would ask me: 'Are you keeping it for when I am dead?' When we were in Munich and visited the architect Frau Troost, the very fashionable widow of Professor Troost, whose opinion Hitler valued highly, he was always anxious that his tie should pass muster.

Decorations from foreign heads of state or the Vatican were anathema to him. He ensured that this was understood after Goebbels was offered a decoration by the Vatican. He liked the idea of becoming a papal chamberlain, as was Franz von Papen. That Hitler allowed himself to be appointed to the honorary rank of corporal in the Fascist militia, which came with the gift of an honour dagger, lay outside this ruling. Apparently he did not wish to risk offending the Italian dictator with whom over the course of time he had begun to establish friendly ties.

Chapter 7

Hitler's Speeches and the Problem of Göring

GÖRING'S PREDILECTION FOR MAGNIFICENT, fantasy uniforms was often the target for Hitler's ridicule. Göring had a unique uniform, most probably designed by himself, for each of his official posts. The most showy of these was his Reichsmarschall's one. His dove-blue tunic with white piping, gold shoulder straps with raised crossed field-marshal's batons and glittering medals outshone everyone in the entourage. He wore the important Spanish Order of the Golden Fleece and broad silky belt on special festive occasions. Less festive but rather more comical was his paratrooper uniform with high boots to above-knee height. He wore this once to a situation conference and I noticed the military men nudging each other with a grin, drawing attention to the comical figure in whispered asides. Hitler stayed aloof from it on this occasion. When he poked fun, he did so openly. He made a cardboard medal for Göring to wear on his nightshirt, and even presented it to him. Whether Göring was amused I never discovered.

It was one of Hitler's annoying and very trying habits to leave the final drafting of his speeches to the very last moment. He would always put the job off if it was at all possible. Once he starting dictating, however, he would dictate the entire speech for his two secretaries to type directly into their machines, often working day and night. While this was going on everything else would take a back seat. As I always noticed that this work, in which he would be totally engrossed, burned up his energy, I once asked him why he did not allow himself more time by starting the dictation much earlier. His answer sounded convincing but tallied only partially with the facts. He explained that he had to delay doing it as long as he could because political events often required a reassessment of the situation, and in such cases he could not allow them to pass without a remark. In actual fact he always knew long in advance what he was going to say. When he had got the draft right in his mind he would walk up and down the room speaking in loud and penetrating tones as if addressing his audience. Each gesture was tried out for its effect. Before him on the table was a clock to time himself. He ignored me completely. Once he had finished dictating to the 'writer-ladies' as he used to call his secretaries, it was my job to take away the typed sheets and get them copied at once. When I returned he would expect me to tarry as he read them aloud, looking at my expression to see whether they 'hung together'. Although aimed at the masses, he liked to get the effect right on individuals.

Often I would be asked if 'the Führer actually composes his own speeches or does Dr Goebbels help him?' I could only say what I knew for sure: Hitler never delegated this task. Goebbels had nothing whatever to do with it. On the contrary: he had to show his own speeches to Hitler, who not infrequently corrected or changed them. Because Hitler's speeches often lasted over an hour, what with all the corrections and rewriting he would usually not complete the task within one working day, especially since the job would not be addressed until the afternoon. At night he would take tablets to help him overcome tiredness and continue working, although by then his secretaries would be totally exhausted and could only keep going with strong coffee. However confident he might have appeared in public, before his speeches he would be nervous, behaving like an anxious actor before going on stage. He would gargle with a mixture of glycerine and water to make his voice 'sound good'. If his speeches extended over two hours or more, as they sometimes tended to do, he feared having an attack of stomach cramps while speaking. Dr Morell used to give him injections beforehand to forestall the stomach problem. As he left the podium he would always be bathed in sweat. It was my job after the speech to wrap Hitler in a thick blanket and escort him home. There he took tablets to prevent getting a chill, drank tea laced with a lot of cognac and took hot baths. When he spoke in a public hall, we tried to keep the temperature at no more than 10–12°C.

Another of his habits of which we failed to cure despite all efforts was the frequency of his requests for the time. We were always hearing 'Linge, what's the time?' or 'Schaub, what time have you got?' or 'Doctor, what does your watch say?' Since this was a nuisance for everybody concerned, we got together at Christmas to buy him a gold watch. He carried it with him for two days. Then 'Linge, what time is it now?' The gift lay unwanted in the drawer of his dresser. Next I got a batch of large clocks and put one in every room so that he could see for himself what the time was. No use: he kept asking. I had the clocks taken away. When in Hitler's presence it was of great importance to know or anticipate his needs. This could not always be inferred from his instructions and orders. 'Thinking aloud' he would bring to light individual problems from all directions and make simple procedures into the most insoluble problems. He presented everything in so convoluted a manner that somebody unfamiliar with his methods would be unable to sort out what he was driving at. He would wander off the subject, talk about irrelevancies and confuse people who were following his explanations closely. Mostly he left it to his listener to put the right 'weight' on a thing and so understand what it was he had been talking about. The military, for example, used to terse and clear orders, had to endure a discourse of one or two hours and they would still be uncertain what he really wanted.

Because of Hitler's style of leadership and government, the 'areas of competence' and jurisdiction of Göring, Goebbels, Hess, Himmler,

Speer, Ribbentrop, Lammers, Meissner and Bormann overlapped, and this caused tensions and jealousies. In Hitler's presence however there had to be no clashes beyond a slightly loud or light sarcastic exchange. As I was spending an increasing period with Hitler I never knew if the rumours about these various personalities, which obviously filtered through to Hitler, were true. For a long time, up to about 1943, one thing for me was certain: Göring was Hitler's most intimate and loyal 'paladin'. He had been at Hitler's side in the attempted putsch of November 1923.

This fact, combined with other shared experiences during the struggle before 1933, and Göring's physical appearance and charisma, which differed so much from Hitler's, seemed to bind the pair of them together and they would frequently speak of their similarities and common path. Hitler saw in Göring, as he often emphasised, the heroic Pour-le-Mérite holder of the First World War, who through his self-confidence and soldierly bearing knew how to command respect. After proving himself a loyal, tough and diplomatic intimate of Hitler as minister-president in Prussia, where he 'created order' to Hitler's concept, he was soon able to substantially enlarge his effective circle thanks to Hitler's custom of weighing down faithful colleagues with more offices and jobs. Göring was given the Luftwaffe to expand, received the forestry and hunting portfolios and all military ventures within the Four Year Plan. Thus not only in political but also in military and economic matters, he was one of Hitler's most influential advisers. I would often see them both wrapped in lively discussions with both temperaments to the fore, contrary to the atmosphere in talks with the military and ministers. That they actually fell out is something I never saw. If Göring's ideas differed from those of Hitler he gave in obediently if Hitler insisted on it.

Even when differences arose between Göring and his minister of aircraft production Ernst Udet, who was responsible for the supply of warplanes, Hitler would not involve himself on Udet's side which was the proper thing for him to do. Göring was simply closer to him. That was typical of Hitler. Whoever enjoyed his confidence remained at the helm even if somebody else was better at steering. Udet had, as was generally felt, experimented too much when the important thing had been to get tested designs into mass production. Udet, unable to get his ideas put through, finally gave up and committed suicide. When Hitler was informed that Udet had shot himself in his aircraft, he was much affected. After reflection he said: 'Pity, that was not the correct thing. Udet should not have given in, but fought for his ideas. He knew that he could come to me at any time.'

Those who knew Hitler understood that he encouraged rivalries, or at least tolerated them, because he wanted to see who came off best. He would stand off and be deaf to complaints and pleas. In the 'natural selection', as he called it, usually he would only interfere when an impasse was reached. Those of weak will, who lacked nerve and endurance, normally had little chance of remaining on top. So it was that the chief of the Luftwaffe general staff, Generaloberst Jeschonnek, also took his own life. Though highly thought of by Hitler, he too had failed to elude his shadow. He had come to grief against the rock of Göring, which reinforced Hitler's view that Göring was the right man for the job. When Göring, tears in his eyes, claimed that Jeschonnek had been 'his best friend', this was too much for Hitler. He reproved him saying that his 'crocodile tears' were not the consequence of true grief and added that 'Jeschonnek could still be alive'.

Göring, who had rejected the plans of both Udet and Jeschonnek, surrounded himself with a staff consisting for the most part of people he had known in the First World War. He ignored the fact that they were unable to adapt to the needs of a modern airforce, as was proved over the course of time. In Hitler's eyes, however, Göring could do something which 'the weak could not': he got his ideas accepted everywhere, and despite all setbacks and difficulties he remained an optimist: even in desperate situations he managed to convince Hitler that the Luftwaffe would be capable of turning the tide.

When the British fled from Dunkirk in 1940 and the idea of pursuit was being considered, Göring reinforced a hesitant Hitler in his decision not to attempt an invasion. The Luftwaffe was always capable of blockading England should that prove necessary, he assured him. Hitler, of the opinion that every British soldier who got back safely was a further 'guarantee' of an early accord with London, was only too happy to hear Göring's promise. But here, as at Stalingrad later, Göring could not deliver.

In my personal experience the following case is typical of Göring's role: in the spring of 1943 at Insterburg in East Prussia a large Luftwaffe air display was held. Amongst many new aircraft the Me 262 jet fighter was to be flown. Göring promised Hitler he would have one thousand jet fighters operational in one year and from 1944 would turn out a further hundred monthly. Yet, at the time of the invasion in June 1944, there were only sixty machines of this type available. 'If I had had only one hundred of these promised jet fighters, the Anglo–American invasion would not have succeeded,' Hitler commented as the Allies were already halfway across France.

Subsequently the swell of voices at Hitler's HQ critical of Göring's leadership grew louder, and even Hitler was no longer able to dismiss it quite so readily as he had been. He ordered Boehm-Tettelbach, one of Göring's former staff officers, to inform him of the situation within the Luftwaffe and resolved to establish the truth of affairs. A team of experts – including aces such as Adolf Galland and Hajo Hermann and leading aircraft manufacturers such as Heinkel and Messerschmitt – were called upon to instruct him in technology and aerial tactics. An immediate programme to produce up to 3,000 aircraft monthly was planned, while the introduction of the V-1 flying bomb and V-2 rocket, which Göring would gladly have handled, was transferred to SS-Gruppenführer Hans Kammler, who in 1945 also took over jet fighter production and operations.

This was a bitter pill for Göring, for the engineer Kammler had been at the Luftwaffe Ministry, where Göring had sidelined him.

Göring's many errors embittered Hitler, who felt deceived and betrayed, and said openly at a situation conference at which Göring was present: 'The only one of you who does not lie to me is Grossadmiral Dönitz.' Nobody protested. Tight-lipped, all accepted this clear and – at least partly – damaging accusation. Göring, whom Hitler had not mentioned by name, was also silent, and I saw how deeply this barb had wounded him. Apparently he thought that he had been unjustly accused.

Amongst the German people, Hermann Göring was the generous, jovial politician with a statesman-like attitude. Hitler knew this and delighted in it. That Göring was actually something different insofar as the term 'jovial' applied was something that I saw constantly. Even Himmler was a more welcome guest for us than Göring. God-like, a Wotan upon his steed, Göring would arrive at Hitler's door, letting slip his cape theatrically from his shoulders, condescending to look around, his eyes and all his gestures commanding his ten to twelve man entourage of flatterers: 'Perceive this event. I am here!' When he stood in the Führer's presence however it all looked different, and was measured by another yardstick. He knew then that he was only a star which shone not by its own light but always needed Hitler's 'sun'. Again and again I saw the crass changes in his demeanour during and after meetings with Hitler, and over and again I saw that Dönitz and Goebbels were men of a different calibre.

So far as I could see they were free of the anxiety which could be perceived distinctly in Göring when he visited Hitler. When he arrived he 'knew' nobody. All his energies were put into a 'show' for the 'domestics' and anybody else he thought fitted into that category by virtue of what job he did, and into sprucing himself for the 'meeting with the Führer' to whom he wished to give the best impression. When Dönitz or Goebbels came, on the other hand, everything was quite different. Dönitz would joke, ask about my family and then say: 'Linge, you scoundrel, announce me to the Führer!' Goebbels was different again, not so much of the old soldier, but had that superiority of manner which the leading National Socialists liked to present in public.

Chapter 8

Goebbels – The Giant in a Dwarf's Body

Y OU COULD TELL GOEBBELS what was on your mind. He would listen, weigh it up and if he thought it useful would then discuss it openly with Hitler. They chatted together – there was nothing forced about their conversations. Once Hitler said after Goebbels had left: 'A giant in a dwarf's body, a man of size!' The genial, small, simple and not very Aryan-looking man had conquered Red Berlin for Hitler, and Hitler sought his company probably because he cast a ray of light over the greyness of his surroundings. Goebbels's lively and amusing conversation spellbound not only all listeners but also Hitler himself. If Goebbels got the better of a guest at the dinner table with his sharp tongue and irony – this would often be Reich press chief Dr Dietrich – he would always manage to extract humour from the situation. Dietrich, the calm and prudent press man, whose private pleasure was angling, allowed all the fireworks to pass over his head without comment, particularly when Hitler was involved in it. Because of his ostentation, Göring was one of Goebbels' favourite and regular targets. Everything about Göring would have tempted a comedian to make a caricature or impersonation. Goebbels portrayed him as a 'Sunday hunter': clad in furs and barricaded into his automobile, he was transported to what he was pleased to call 'the wild' and there set up his rifle with telescopic sight in the forked branch of a tree. Hitler, who did not have a high opinion of amateur hunters and preferred the courage of the hunter-trapper, took pleasure in hearing this criticism of his Reich hunt-master.

Although Hitler did not always excel in the selection of his colleagues, in Goebbels he had found a man who filled the office of propaganda minister in masterly fashion. He was 'a direct hit', as Hitler once said. When Goebbels addressed thousands, all hung on his words and were equally fascinated and convinced by him as were we who sat around him in a small circle. In addition to these capabilities there was another part of his character which Hitler liked to stress: Goebbels had courage, steadfastness and the will to see things through. At table Goebbels liked to reminisce about the 'hall brawls' during the period of struggle, a subject that in times of crisis was seized upon as a 'heartener'. In Berlin, where the Rhinelander Goebbels felt at his best, he was known as 'the little doctor', a term which was in no way derogatory. Everybody knew that like few others before 1933, he had proven his courage and cunning. That these qualities were inherent in his personality I was often able to observe for myself.

Goebbels was not frightened to bring to light improprieties resulting from abuses committed by Party members. He reported to Hitler quite candidly on irregularities in the state medical funds, a sector in which SA people had risen to key positions after the seizure of power. When they were unable to justify the trust placed in them, Goebbels stepped in, and after Hitler declined to act Goebbels appealed to the Party court and won. Goebbels cleaned up the pigsties where the old cronies held sway and put a stop to the orgies. That he did not spare his old comrades spoke well for him. Those who were disciplined and considered that their wings had been clipped against the Führer's wishes, staging a protest outside the Propaganda Ministry, ran into an obstacle of granite. Hitler fell in behind Goebbels, who would not allow himself to be intimidated. When important posts came up in future, in my presence I heard Hitler order that though old Party members were still to be considered for the vacancies, if they were not suited there were other areas where they could be put without breaking the china. Later, when Hitler spoke on this subject, he said that Atatürk, the Turkish statesman, would have agreed that initially Hitler had given too much preference to old comrades and put too many of them into jackets that did not fit. Realising this, he would frequently justify himself by saying: 'I have Gauleiters who come from simple backgrounds, but who discharge their duties satisfactorily.' Actually it was so: the man who did 'his incompetent best' would not be ejected from office simply for his failure to shine.

Hitler acknowledged the value of Goebbels as a propagandist to his closest circle, where he often would not spare the blushes in being blunt. On the other hand, he did not always approve of Goebbels's private life. The many little stories circulating about Goebbels concerned him deeply. Because radio, the theatre and the film industry all came under the Propaganda Ministry, Goebbels often came into contact with actresses and other female artistes upon whom the minister – and perhaps even more so the genial talker who could help one get ahead in one's career – often made a lasting impression. I often noticed how artistes and starlets of film and theatre would swarm around him, rivals for his favour. Goebbels – of whom Hitler secretly wished 'if only he had two healthy legs and feet' – had no armour against female wiles, and love affairs were the consequence.

A scandal erupted when the beautiful Czech film star Lída Baarová entered his adoring circle. She exercised such a spell over Goebbels that he quite lost his head and almost wrecked his until then happy marriage with wife Magda. His Secretary of State, Karl Hanke, the personal confidante who knew about Goebbels's affairs, was a person who held Frau Goebbels in the highest regard and was thus at a loss to know which road he should now follow. He came and asked me 'to arrange a date to see the Führer', which I did, and now Hitler discovered what lay behind all the rumours. Frau

Goebbels wanted a divorce and to emigrate to Switzerland, causing Hitler to envisage for himself a major scandal. He decided to attempt a reconciliation of the couple and invited them both to Obersalzberg. There he received them separately. In individual conversations he explained to them that they must relegate their personal interests to those of the state. The separation was prevented. In the Berghof Great Hall he made them both promise to remain loyal to each other from now on. Happy at having resolved the crisis he brought the reconciled couple himself to the NSDAP guesthouse on Obersalzberg and wished them jokingly 'a happy second honeymoon'.

He did not wish to be reminded of this particular episode in future. That I did so once by accident he graciously overlooked. It was amongst my duties to place before Hitler those photographs of him that the press and illustrated magazines wanted to publish. I had this task to do shortly before 20 April 1944, his fifty-fifth birthday. As always, I separated out beforehand the photographs that he did not wish to see: pictures of certain localities or personalities. In my haste I had not noticed that one of them showing Hitler and Goebbels surrounded by artistes at the Neubabelsberg film studio included Lída Baarová near Goebbels. Hitler returned it to me with a smile: 'I don't think we ought to have that one.'

That Goebbels attempted to turn Hitler against Göring I saw from early on. I wondered at the thinly disguised enmity between the 'little doctor' and 'Hermann', equally beloved amongst the people, most of whom were even prepared to forgive him for the poor showing of the Luftwaffe. Since Hitler constantly parried Goebbels's attacks against Göring and refused to draw the conclusions that the Reich propaganda minister considered unavoidable, at first I thought it must be based on private jealousies, quarrels and rivalries. In the course of time, particularly after the Allied invasion, I got to know better. Around mid-March 1945 I heard Goebbels informing the Führer in his mournful sing-song tones that Göring had utterly failed and that the future of the German people depended on an incapable Reichsmarschall no longer able 'to make the Luftwaffe led by himself into a powerful instrument'. He spoke of corruption, of absolutely essential changes that had to be made in the Luftwaffe general staff and of a debit balance in this respect that Göring could no longer repay because of the state into which the Luftwaffe had fallen. I thought this over. Outwardly there was unblemished unity, confidence and 'trust in God'. Behind the scenes and at the levers of power, where I was a constant onlooker, things looked rather different. What the Propaganda Ministry could not admit publicly was that the Führer had a shadow he could not outwit. Hitler hesitated and procrastinated and gave in to personal prejudices with regard to Göring even though he seemed to sense that he had to act in the matter eventually. With drooping shoulders and dragging-limping steps Goebbels left the discussion in which he had achieved nothing.

Hitler, who had violently criticised Göring in 1942 for the failure of the Luftwaffe, causing him to cast aside all his decorations and awards, could still not, despite all the evidence of failure, decide to swing the axe. The defeat at Stalingrad worked in Göring's favour, even though a large part of the blame for it must be laid at his door. The result was that, even though he should have been replaced, he was not, as Hitler so distrusted the army after Stalingrad that he could not cut adrift an old, proven fighter like Göring.

At this late stage of the war Hitler drew him much closer than previously, showing him emphatically that he was still needed. I could see here how feelings and memories overruled common sense. Apparently he had convinced himself that the regenerated Göring could be once again the cunning old fighter with whom he had marched to the Feldherrnhalle in November 1923 and who had fallen wounded. When I once reported to Hitler before the Stalingrad disaster that Göring was waiting to be received as a guest, he had replied most rudely that he could expect no special consideration since even the Reichsmarschall had to eat the same stew as he,

Hitler, and the other guests did. Now, after the catastrophe, he was suddenly caring about Göring, inviting him to dine and asking him if there might not be something he could prepare especially for him. This revived concern finally convinced Göring to forget his difficult situation, and soon he was bringing along his own recipes and a beer specially brewed for himself.

During the war Goebbels only visited FHQ when summoned there by Hitler. In the 1941 winter crisis, when the people were asked to contribute towards winter clothing for troops at the front, I was present at a discussion between Hitler and Goebbels in which the minister maintained insistently that Moscow would have fallen if only ten per cent more troops had been used. Total war had been necessary here, he emphasised. Hitler replied that he had been opposed because at that time he had not then wished to inflict the burden of total war on the German people. It was impressive, and not only for me, that Goebbels was much more firm and committed on this than Hitler. If Hitler had given in, total war would certainly have begun in the winter of 1941. Not only by the instance above did Goebbels show that he did not belong amongst Hitler's yes-men. Often he had the courage to say 'no' and would make criticisms in Hitler's presence where nobody else would dare to do so. On a trip I once heard him say: 'Unfortunately the Führer has too many sentence-finishers around him.' He said this so loudly and clearly that Hitler had to hear it, and I saw that he heard. When the Reich Chancellery became the FHQ in 1945, Goebbels was Hitler's closest confidante. After the military situation conferences I was constantly sent by Hitler to fetch Goebbels for conversations which would usually be hours long. Much of what Goebbels confided to his diary I heard with my own ears.

Chapter 9

Himmler and Bormann

T
HE THIRD PERSONALITY MOST mentioned in connection
with Hitler is Heinrich Himmler. He had been a student,
military ensign and an agriculturalist before joining the
NSDAP and Hitler after a brief career with a Freikorps. Himmler
had started out as Gregor Strasser's secretary in Lower Bavaria. His
origins, education and interest, his anti-semitic 'world-view' and
his enthusiastic schemes to improve the world recommended him
straightaway for the post Hitler was to give him. At Hitler's order he
was to organise and expand the SS, the so-called 'protection staff' of
the Party. It was to become a Party militia on military lines dedicated
to Hitler through thick and thin. As chief of the Party-SS Himmler
came to Hitler's notice early on account of his pedantic reliability,
'fulfilment of duty' and talent for organisation. Himmler was setting
out to realise what he had dreamed of, if only indistinctly, for years.
He would lead an elite: men who impressed by their physical build
and were so far as possible 'perfect racial specimens'. Hitler's idea
that this 'Order of the Death's Head', as Heinz Höhne later called
the SS, should receive not only careful military training but also have
a systematic National Socialist background through indoctrination
corresponded exactly to Himmler's intentions. That in practice it
did not quite reach this standard I noticed for myself. When I came
to Hitler in 1935 I knew about as much about National Socialism
as any other soldier of the same age in the Wehrmacht. Although
it lacked a detailed understanding of the 'world-view', the military

training of the SS could be used for special missions which the Wehrmacht would almost certainly have rejected, and thus it met the expectations of Hitler and Himmler for which it had been created.

General conversations between Hitler and Himmler before the war were not always held behind closed doors. I was thus witness to many of their talks and would always keep a keen ear for when they spoke about the *SS-Leibstandarte*, my own unit. When the SS won its first laurels on the battlefield alongside the German army, Himmler, very conscious of history, tried to introduce a system of knighthoods for SS men who had proved especially valiant. This 'nobility', which to Himmler's idea should not be hereditary, struck Hitler as a fantasy and to Himmler's disappointment declined to proceed with it. The Reichsführer had already worked out all the procedures down to the minutest detail. The document bestowing nobility was to be inserted into the hilt of the SS dagger and always carried on the battlefield. The members of this Order were obliged to marry the 'racially most valuable women' and thus he would have the offspring on a lead from cradle to grave. Hitler, who had his own ideas about healthy heredity, heard Himmler out and then condemned the idea as 'playing at sandcastles'.

One day Hitler's travelling physician Karl Brandt came and proposed that the women whom SS officers wanted to marry should be obliged beforehand to qualify for marriage by winning the Reich sports badge. Hitler asked me: 'Linge, what's your mother's best time for the hundred metres?' When I said I did not know he said cheerfully: 'My mother didn't have a sport badge either, but nevertheless I think I turned out to be quite a good German.'

Hitler also rejected Himmler's plan to replace Christianity with the old Germanic gods and the cults of Wotan and Thor. For him it was sufficient that the SS had no ties to a Church. When Hitler and Mussolini were lunching alone on Obersalzberg one day, Hitler brought the talk round to the subject of religion. The conversation rambled in general terms over the question of the Vatican and the

Church. Hitler pointed out that not only the Italian royal house was causing the Duce difficulties but also the Church, which was why it was necessary for Mussolini to react and 'explain things' to the people. When the Duce shook his giant head lightly from side to side and asked by his stare how that was to be achieved in Italy, of all places, Hitler said to me in an aside: 'Linge, do you go to church? How many men of my SS bodyguard and the *Leibstandarte* attend services?' I told him the truth: 'None, mein Führer'. This hit Mussolini literally like a low blow. He stared at me speechless with large eyes. Hitler lapped up this enjoyable little scene.

Himmler was a calm, unimpressive and self-possessed man. I never knew him to commit any act of violence himself but without a moment's reflection he would issue orders of such to be carried out by others. To us in Hitler's staff he appeared inscrutable. We had no affection for him and liked it better when he was departing than arriving. We also knew that he imposed drastic punishments on SS men for even the most minor infractions. The kind of rules he set were unbelievable. In the SS it was forbidden to eat salted potatoes. Potatoes also had to be cooked unpeeled. If he noticed that somebody was looking thin or pale he would award him a ban on smoking for twenty-four hours to the minute. Hitler would often poke fun at these goings-on but made no attempt to intervene because the SS was loyal to Himmler. He even left to Himmler the decision on marriage applications from SS men wanting to marry foreign girls, a power that even extended into the Wehrmacht.

Whether Himmler ever held grudges I was unable to determine. If somebody was off form he would remember his past errors, but these would not necessarily be taken into account in determining disciplinary punishments. When the Führer looked over some of Himmler's detailed instructions on one occasion he joked: 'Himmler is a pedant like his father. Really an ideal man for Reich culture minister' – and then after a brief pause – 'But I need him where he is.'

The extent of his complicity I discovered only after the war, for Hitler only discussed with him in absolute privacy that of which I would never have believed Himmler capable – the mass annihilation of the Jews. Himmler issued the orders to kill the Jews although he would have found it against the grain to kill anyone by his own hand. It did not surprise me at all to learn, after 1945, that he would be inflexible in his punishment of any SS man who looted a corpse, for example. For the office with which Hitler had entrusted him he was probably the right man, but not the right man for the job. If somebody else had been in his shoes possibly much less might have been done. Himmler had no First World War front experience, which put him in a particularly inferior position as regards Hitler. He was always having to 'prove' himself, and I often saw and heard how Hitler treated him when nobody else was about. Then Himmler would no longer be the 'almighty' Reichsführer, but a recruit on the parade ground.

In the Gestapo and SD there was much of his personality. Hitler often used to bemoan the fact that there had been nothing similar to the SD in the First World War. He read the reports of this intelligence organisation even when he was overloaded with work. That they were not flattering did not disturb him, for through them he reckoned he knew the morale in the country better than anyone. It said much for Himmler's organisational abilities on which Hitler was dependent to some extent that he structured the Gestapo in such a manner that nobody outside it ever knew anything about it.

I knew that after 1933 many people had been sent to concentration camps. As I understood it, the inmates were all opponents of National Socialism or convicted felons. I often discovered, sometimes from Hitler himself, when political detainees were being released. The important consideration here was the belief that they would not act illegally after being set free. Himmler told me that the leaders of the main opposition parties could secure their release by signing a pledge not to engage in political activities in future. Many well-known social democrats and communists accepted, which seemed to surprise Hitler. I remember particularly the leader of the German Communist Party, Torgler, who unlike Ernst Thälmann was prepared to sign the pledge. He was released and took up work as a journalist, which spoke for itself. During the campaign in Russia, of his own free will Torgler wrote a letter to Hitler which he passed to me to read. Torgler wrote that his son was on the Eastern Front as a soldier and that the conditions that the Russian people had had to endure under Stalin's dictatorship had appalled him. Torgler's letter closed with the assurance that what his son reported had so affected him that he, the father, had renounced communism once and for always and had been cured of his earlier beliefs. Hitler was very pleased with this letter and said: 'We should send all German communists to the Soviet Union so that they can see the paradise for themselves.' Thälmann, who refused to renounce communism or abandon political activities for communism if released, remained in a concentration camp until his violent end in 1944,* but interested Hitler, Himmler and Göring to the last. They did not actually concern themselves about him, of course, but Hitler mentioned the name occasionally and asked several times how Thälmann was getting along. When Himmler spoke to Thälmann on a visit to the camp, Thälmann made a suggestion that Himmler relayed to Hitler at Thälmann's express request. Hitler should award a special medal to the most able workers in the armaments industry, he said. Hitler, in whom such ideas were not lacking, was surprised. He stared at Himmler, shook his head and decided to try it out. The first German worker to receive the Knights' Cross of the War Service Cross (Ritterkreuz zum Kreigsverdienstkreuz) was named Ritter.

---

* Ernst Thälmann, leader of the German Communist Party (KPD) was arrested by the Gestapo in 1933 after advocating the violent overthrow of the National Socialist state. He was held in solitary confinement at Bautzen Prison until August 1944, when he was transferred to Buchenwald and shot on Hitler's orders on 18 August. (TN)

What went on in the concentration camps during the war remained – as they did to everybody in Hitler's circle – a mystery. The conferences in this respect between Hitler and Himmler were held in private. For us, Himmler was the man behind the scenes. Not until my spell in Soviet captivity did I discover that gas chambers and ovens had been installed in the camps. It may appear rather incredible, but during my service with Hitler I knew nothing of the dreadful events which were to provoke such outrage throughout the world. Repeatedly I have heard it said that Hitler could not have known everything. That is pure nonsense. True, I was not present when Hitler and Himmler discussed these things – nobody else was there – but I know from personal observation and Hitler's remarks that he knew everything. I was often on hand when, with sparkling eyes and trembling voice, he would say that he would rid himself ruthlessly of anybody who opposed him. There was no possibility of any misunderstanding in this. I would not have known him if I believed that all he really meant by that was loss of freedom. For him it was clear that 'the ends justified the means'.

Martin Bormann also came from the ranks of the old NSDAP membership. Like Himmler he had also worked on the land. Under Rudolf Hess he had exercised the function of Party head of staff. Outwardly he no more resembled the physical image which National Socialism prized than Himmler or Goebbels. In stature he was of small build, fat and robust, an uncouth and unbelievably hyperactive personality. Whatever he did was carried through with unscrupulous force. He crushed underfoot anybody in his path. He was one of those persons for whom you instinctively stand even if you met him as a stranger in the street. His close personal relationship to Hitler, at which he was working doggedly when I joined Hitler's staff, was achieved by enlarging Hitler's country house Wachenfeld on Obersalzberg. He arranged finance for this endeavour skilfully by diverting Party funds and gave Hitler, who had no real understanding

Linge with Hitler at the Wolf's Lair, the Führer's Eastern Front headquarters near the East Prussian town of Rastenburg, in 1942.

Above: Hitler and his entourage en route to the Reichstag on the eve of war. Behind Hitler sits Linge (middle row), Joseph Goebbels (back row left) and Robert Ley, head of the German Labour Front.

Below: Linge posted at the door of the railway carriage in the Compiègne Forest, at the scene of the French armistice in June 1940. He is standing next to the French General Huntziger and Ambassador Noël.

Above: The inner circle in discussions at the Wolf's Lair. Hitler walks with Albert Bormann (left) and Martin Bormann (right), Hitler's private secretary and the head of the Nazi Party Chancellery, with Linge following behind.

Below: A triumphant Hitler greets members of the Luftwaffe in the spring of 1940, when the German war machine seemed unstoppable. Linge, with goggles, stands behind the Führer.

Above: Italian leader Benito Mussolini is greeted by Hitler at the Wolf's Lair in the summer of 1941. Mussolini continued to visit the headquarters after he was deposed, including the day of the 20 July plot of 1944. Linge stands to the left of the picture.

Below: Hitler and Mussolini inspect the recently deployed Italian troops on the Ukrainian frontline, August 1941.

At the Wolf's Lair in 1942
Above *(from left): Albert Bormann, Linge, Hitler, Albert Speer*
Below *(from left): Linge, Albert Bormann, Hitler and Julius Schaub, Hitler's chief aide*

*At the end of June
1943, talks were held
in Salzburg to discuss
Italian military failures
and the danger of an
Allied invasion of Italy.
Right (from left): Linge,
Hitler, Otto Meissner,
Albert Bormann,
Hermann Göring and
Walther Hewel
Below (from left): Albert
Bormann, Linge, Hitler,
unidentified, Hewel,
Joachim von Ribbentrop
and Meissner*

One of the last known photographs of Hitler, taken on 20 March 1945 in the garden of the Reich Chancellery in Berlin. From left: Hitler Youth leader Artur Axmann, Hermann Fegelein, Julius Schaub, Hitler, General Wilhelm Burgdorf and Linge

Left: Linge shortly before his release after ten years of Soviet captivity. Though he was sentenced to twenty-five years imprisonment, Linge was released early in the general amnesty of 1955.

Below: Linge holds telegrams with offers for the publication of his memoirs upon his return to Germany in 1955.

of money, the feeling that here was somebody who might relieve him of all the burdens in this area with which he did not wish to be encumbered. When more structures went up on Obersalzberg later, we were not really surprised to see that Bormann himself had now acquired a magnificent country house and wormed himself into Hitler's close personal circle on the basis of being his 'neighbour'. Bormann was a strong personality whose influence even on Hitler I had occasion to remark often. He worked day and night, allowed colleagues and employees no rest and tyrannised them. For the most minor error he would ruthlessly cull a member of staff. He called for a furious work rate and appalled not only his workers and advisers but his adjutants such as Hühner too. His fitting nickname was 'The Lord God of Obersalzberg'.

During the French campaign I saw an episode that betrayed his character and nature. He had an assistant in Dr Heinrich Heim whose serenity stood in stark contrast to that of his master. After Heim had again infuriated Bormann with his unshakeable calm, and withstood a raging diatribe, Heim turned to me impassively and said in a voice that Bormann could not avoid hearing: 'You see, Herr Linge, he comes from the land. Before this he only had contact with animals. One must therefore overlook it when he roars so loudly.' Hitler, who was told about this, laughed and promised 'little Heim' as he called him, whose knowledge of art he esteemed highly, the post of his personal librarian once the war was over.

Bormann's wife was the daughter of Reichsleiter Buch, the president of the Supreme Party Court. Through this marriage, Bormann, who outwardly behaved as though he was not interested in personal advancement, infiltrated the Party leadership. As a husband and father he was a tyrant. It was an open secret on the Berg that in moments of uncontrolled rage he would resort to physical violence against his wife and children. Since a large family was considered exemplary, Frau Bormann had girded herself to bear ten children. This quiet and modest woman, whose life can have been no bed of roses under her violent and ill-tempered spouse, was literally the slave of a power-hungry egoist who had lovers and denied his wife the standing and respect she merited.

He determined when and how long she was allowed to be Hitler's guest at the Berghof. Mainly she was restricted to the film shows after supper. When the film ended and the guests sat around in free conversation she would be dismissed from the house at a signal from her husband. Sometimes she would receive this signal prematurely and have to leave during the film. Basically Bormann did not want to see her around after ten at night. Silent, depressed and clearly upset, she would try to steal away unnoticed.

The much-vaunted 'high life on Obersalzberg' was not to be found at Hitler's Berghof, but in Bormann's country house. I mention it here only in passing. Before the war only New Year was celebrated at the Berghof in a big way. Bormann threw his own seasonal parties. His guests were principally film actresses who interested him personally. Cruelly, his wife had to do all the arranging and chores, but was not permitted to circulate. On one such occasion he dragged her out of bed at midnight to go into Munich for him to fetch a shirt for his dresscoat.

As a result of his constant attendance upon Hitler, Bormann developed a greater insight into Hitler's way of thinking than anybody else. He spared Hitler not only a great deal of work but unburdened him of irritations such as the Gauleiter conferences. Bormann took these over and reported to the Party leadership corps afterwards on what had been discussed. When the war began, Bormann's office had been enlarged to such an extent that he was constantly at FHQ as the Party's liaison man.

After Hess made his sensational flight to Britain in May 1941, it was obvious to Hitler that Bormann should be Hess's successor. Thus Bormann rose to be Hitler's deputy in the Party and later decided to call himself 'The Führer's Secretary' for the sake of simplicity. That he was soon much more than that is proved by numerous facts.

He had created for himself a position of power that no general or minister could afford to ignore. Every document was subjected to his scrutiny before it reached Hitler, and thus he could exercise his plenipotentiary powers. Hitler found Bormann's tireless work rate a great help. Often he would emphasise his recognition of it: 'The Party's apparatus of command has never worked better.' No wonder, for every wish and gesture of Hitler's was interpreted by Bormann as a command. Important bulletins, for example about air raids, the damage inflicted and the emergency measures necessary, reached Hitler quicker through Bormann's Party chancellery than through the official report channels. Bormann built a wall around Hitler which made it impossible even for Gauleiters and Reichsleiters to approach him.

When the war entered its final stage in 1944 and the Volkssturm was formed, Bormann gained his first official foothold in the military sector. He attended the situation conferences and gave the military the impression that he was ubiquitous and indispensable for the Führer. For some time he had been waging a secret war against the military, whose influence had expanded because of the war causing Bormann to suspect that this might diminish the power of the Party. Thus he was chained to Hitler, had to remain with him to the end, and in his attempt to escape from Berlin after Hitler's suicide met his own death.

Chapter 10

Hess's Mysterious Mission
– Was Hitler Behind It?

RUDOLF HESS WAS A completely different kind of personality. Born at Alexandria, Egypt, he had been imprisoned with Hitler at Landsberg in 1923/4 and at Hitler's dictation had typed out the manuscript for *Mein Kampf* with his forefingers. Anybody could talk to him. He would listen to an argument, consider it and then decide, calmly and impartially, on its merits to the best of his knowledge and conscience. He was never one for whispers and intrigues, and nobody could say that Hess 'the Führer's deputy' ever deliberately set out to hurt anyone. He was distinguished by his many human qualities. His whims, his capricious moods, his belief in astrology, his strange diet and his musings counted against him for little. We all loved him. All the more shocked we were, therefore, to learn of his mysterious flight to Britain on the morning of 11 May 1941.

At 0930 that morning, Hess's adjutant Karl-Heinz Pintsch and Bormann's brother Albert came to me in a state of some excitement and requested that I 'please waken the Führer at once'. They had, Albert Bormann said, 'a very important message from Hess for the Führer.' Because Hitler had stayed awake until very late and had ordered me expressly not to waken him before midday, I refused their request. Pintsch went slack and kept shifting his weight from one foot to the other. 'So, what's up? What do you wish to report to the Führer?' I enquired. Pintsch blurted out: 'Hess has left Germany in the aircraft.' I felt the ground open beneath me. I went at once to Hitler's door and knocked. After a few moments Hitler asked: 'What is it, Linge?' With a trembling voice I reported what Pintsch had said, and that he had a letter from Hess to deliver. Before I had recovered my composure Hitler appeared in the open doorway fully dressed and shaved. I suspected at once that he must have had a premonition. There was no other way to explain how he came to be dressed and waiting in his bedroom at 0930 after giving me express orders not to get him out of bed until midday.[1]

I summoned Pintsch to hand Hess's letter to Hitler. 'Do you know the contents of this letter?' Hitler asked peremptorily. When Pintsch admitted that he did, Hitler sent for RSD chief Peter Högl who placed Pintsch under arrest and took him away. 'I had him arrested,' Hitler said, 'not because he knows what Hess wrote but for not informing me immediately of Hess's preparations. Who is the Führer, Hess or I?'

That Pintsch was also sworn to loyalty and obedience to his immediate superior Hess was of no interest to Hitler at this moment. With an impassive expression he ordered Bormann and von Ribbentrop to appear before him. They were equally surprised. He summoned Göring himself. Lending his voice a 'dramatic' tone he said, 'Göring, something terrible has happened.' There was an

---

1 Hitler's army adjutant Gerhard Engel puts this incident differently. He stated in *Heeresadjutant Bei Hitler 1938–1943* (Stuttgart 1974, p.103) that he had just made a report to Hitler when Albert Bormann appeared and told him that Pintsch wanted to give Hitler a very important letter from Hess, which then happened. Linge dismisses the Engel version as incorrect. (TN): Historian Erich Kern (in Kempka & Kern, *Die Letzten Tage mit Adolf Hitler*, DVG Preussisch-Oldendorf 1991, p.12) commented of the Engel diaries that there might have been an extraneous, that is Allied, influence at work in their compilation post war insofar as passages were omitted and long sections of text very critical of Hitler's leadership inserted. Moreover original handwritten notes were missing, and on the historiographic evidence alone, e.g. comparison with the 6. Armee files, the Engel diaries were not contemporaneous.

awful atmosphere. Everybody tried to stay clear of Hitler. I could not avoid him, and saw that he appeared surprised, concerned and angry only in the presence of others. I did not dare ask if he knew of Hess's flight to Britain, but his behaviour told me that he not only knew in advance but had also probably sent Hess to Britain himself in order to broker an arrangement between London and Berlin through Lord Hamilton, whom Hess had got to know at the Berlin Olympics.

Officially Hitler denied this on 13 June 1941 at the Berghof before sixty or seventy senior civil servants, ministers, Gauleiters, and so on. He asserted that Hess was mentally ill and had put the Reich in an embarrassing situation through his 'crazy idea'. Too much hinted that he only said this because Hess's mission had failed, however. Instinctively I recalled how a few days before the event he had held a conversation with Hess lasting about four hours, which was extraordinary, for it was the first such conference between them since the outbreak of war. Whatever had been discussed remains a mystery. They understood each other and knew the most likely way to achieve their aims.

Another pointer to Hitler's 'complicity' in my opinion was his reprimand to Martin Bormann, following a complaint by Frau Hess, after Bormann had promptly renamed two of his children, Rudolf and Ilse, named for their godparents Rudolf and Ilse Hess.

Hess, who had been a test pilot for Messerschmitt, had parachuted down near Lord Hamilton's Scottish castle Dungavel from a long-range Me-110 fighter-bomber equipped with two 900-litre supplementary tanks (in addition to the inbuilt standard 1200-litre tanks) supplied by his old friend Willi Messerschmitt. The news came through quickly that under interrogation by Lord Simon, Hess had stated that he had come to Britain without Hitler's knowledge. Thus his version coincided with Hitler's.

As I observed Hitler closely another thing that surprised me was his failure to have Gauleiter Ernst Wilhelm Bohle, head of the NSDAP Overseas organisation, arrested. Bohle had translated into

English for Hess the letter of thanks to be given to Lord Hamilton in Britain. Hitler merely asked Bohle in a loud voice and with theatrical anger in front of the assembled 'team' if he 'were mad as well'. All those present froze at this performance. All were awaiting an unrestrained outburst of fury until Göring intervened in a scene that had every appearance of being staged. Hitler had advanced towards Bohle with arms half raised, asking him threateningly if he had 'gone crazy'. Göring asked the Gauleiter in an impassive voice to tell the Führer quietly what he knew and had done. At this Hitler immediately calmed down, taking Bohle aside for a talk and showed him the Hess letter which Pintsch had brought. There was between ten to fifteen pages of it, typed by his secretary Laura Schrödl, and it contained a different basis for the 'operation', which according to Pintsch's later information had gone wrong once before in January 1941. That Himmler knew nothing – and everything pointed to this – did not surprise me. In Hitler's opinion, this affair was too big for him, at least at this time.

With the sudden disappearance of Hess, Martin Bormann's hour had come. He reacted with glee to the report that Hess had flown to Britain. He observed to Hitler with malice: 'He must have gone mad. Flies to Britain, parachutes down and hopes to meet friends with whom he can work out a political deal.' I asked myself how Bormann knew that Hess had used a parachute: Hitler's silence on the point surprised me. His later explanation that in the way of things Lord Hamilton could not admit to 'having known Hess' fed more doubts about the 'surprise' which Hess had dished up to him. Another thing suggesting Hitler's involvement in the episode was his statement that, if the British public had found out what Hess was proposing to say and negotiate, the British government would have been placed in an extremely difficult position because the Opposition would not have wished to continue with the war.

Bormann at least, who condemned Hess as a traitor and said he should be executed if he were ever repatriated during the war, was not unprepared. Since the summer of 1939 he had been continually forcing himself into the foreground. We often had the impression that Hess stayed away from the Reich Chancellery because Bormann's 'politics', the aim of which was apparently to unseat him, were so offensive. The atmosphere on Obersalzberg changed overnight in May 1941. Hitler now used Bormann, but kept him at a distance. He had always considered Hess to be an equal: Bormann was just a servant on whom he could rely, and Hitler treated him as such.

In Russia, Soviet officers told me that Hess was 'crazy', and that he was a 'crazy man' in Spandau Prison, where he had been sentenced to atone 'for his crimes' for the rest of his life. They asked me what I knew about him from my own experience, his influence on Hitler and 'if he had always been crazy'. Certainly, Hitler had declared him to be mentally unwell in May 1941. My explanation that after Hess flew to Britain Hitler had had no option but to say this they accepted immediately, to my surprise, which made me wonder until it became clear what they wanted. They were seeking confirmation that the Western Allies had saved Hess from the noose at Nuremberg because when in London he had tried to win over the British and Americans for a joint war with Hitler against the Soviets. What was I supposed to say to that? I said nothing. I could admit with a clear conscience, however, that in the normal sense of the term Hess had always been sane.

I could well imagine how Hess had led them all a merry dance at Nuremberg. He had remained inscrutable throughout and knew how to cultivate that impression. Often it was difficult to know if Hess were joking or speaking seriously. He always looked like a soldier on duty, and if he ever dropped this deportment, cast off his lugubrious, laconic attitude and told a joke, somebody who did not know him might actually think at that moment that Hess was not quite normal. Thus in the middle of a conference it would suddenly occur to him to position a chair in such a way that he could suddenly make a standing jump over it or perhaps raise it with his legs, stretch out his arms to clasp it and holding the chair in his hands do several knee bends. He would not care who was present. The preesence of Goebbels, Himmler, Göring and other Party and state bosses did not bother him. Only if Hitler were there did he desist.

Chapter 11

Other Leading Personalities and the Eternal Stomach Problem

ONE OF THE FEW 'greats' not to come from amongst the early Party members was Joachim von Ribbentrop. Married into the famous Henkell champagne family, he met Hitler for the first time in 1932 at the Berghof. They were so quickly of one mind that Hitler paid a return call on Ribbentrop at Berlin Dahlem in January 1933.

Oskar von Hindenburg (the son of the Reich president), von Papen (the Reich Chancellor), von Ribbentrop and Hitler met to prepare Hitler as chancellor, as became known immediately afterwards. Ribbentrop's role in this game was greatly appreciated by Hitler even later. Although the intolerable arrogance of his foreign minister aggravated him, he was prepared to overlook it. 'He has already made himself a great store of merit', he once murmured when Ribbentrop kept him waiting an age before coming to the telephone. Not far behind Göring in vanity, it appeared that he had remarkable political ability. Hitler sent him to London as ambassador and subsequently gave him the Foreign Ministry as the successor to von Neurath. In Hitler's mind this position put Ribbentrop close to the highest level of leadership in ranking. Ribbentrop loved pomp and expensive glitter. In London, throwing money around, he made the German Embassy into something approaching a palace. Whoever mentioned this to Hitler received the reply that Germany must have worthy representation of her greatness and strength through her ambassadors abroad and that it was a false economy to want to make savings there. It was quite inappropriate, he counselled critics, for the representatives of the Reich to have to 'eat their way' from one state banquet to the next, as had been the case with the Weimar Republic. Despite Ribbentrop's ambition and careerism, it had been von Neurath who had failed Hitler by not introducing a 'cleansing action' amongst the officials and employees at the Foreign Ministry as Hitler had wanted. After Ribbentrop had succeeded von Neurath as Reich foreign minister, he had tried to warm himself under Hitler's sun and be seen often in his presence. Hitler let him hoof the ground in annoyance. Often I would hear Hitler snap: 'First put your ministry in order.' For his policies towards Britain, Hitler admitted freely, Ribbentrop had been the right man from the beginning. 'In Ribbentrop', he stated, full of hope after appointing him foreign minister, 'I have found the obstinate man with whom I can confront the obstinate British.'

Ribbentrop was very arrogant in his manner. This brought him into opposition with Göring and Goebbels, both of whom were free of it despite their high offices. After Ribbentrop had 'cleansed' his ministry in the manner required by Hitler and renewed his attempts to create for himself a special power base, he came into conflict with Goebbels. Ribbentrop had built his own press office for propaganda, which trespassed into Goebbels's territory. The matter was referred to Hitler for a decision. Ribbentrop lost out. 'Ribbentrop, kindly do your best with the previously existing installation', Hitler told him and added, 'we already have a Propaganda Ministry,'

Ribbentrop's nature can be demonstrated by the following incident. On the occasion of Hitler's fiftieth birthday in April 1939, a march past was held on the large Heer-Strasse in Berlin. The Czechoslovak president, Hacha, and von Neurath, the former foreign minister and now Reich Protector of Bohemia and Moravia, were invited as guests. Protocol demanded that von Neurath should have a more prominent position that Ribbentrop, who protested indignantly. He felt slighted and complained to Hitler. As Reich Protector, von Neurath counted as a head of state, Hitler explained, and on such occasions ranked beside the Führer himself.

Ribbentrop's exaggerated need for recognition often led to friction. His arrogance did not stop at Hitler. Occasionally Ribbentrop made him wait on the line until it pleased the foreign minister to come to the receiver. Hitler spoke to him on this subject but Ribbentrop took no notice. During the war, Ribbentrop and Goebbels had to set up their offices in the Hotel Kaiserhof because of the lack of space. Ribbentrop demanded so much room for the Foreign Ministry that Goebbels put its entire contents out on the street. The expansion of the ministry prompted Hitler to remark after the fall of France: 'Note that after the weapons fall silent, we will not be needing a Foreign Ministry any more.' He also reminded Ribbentrop of the statement by the Italian foreign minister Count Ciano, who after Italy entered the war had said: 'I am shutting down my ministry to become an airman.' After the declaration of 'total war', Ribbentrop considered himself exempt from the order to release all those liable for conscription for service at the front. When Hitler heard this he asked to see the Foreign Ministry personnel lists. Upon observing that Ribbentrop was retaining more staff than was necessary, he sent for him and delivered a reprimand. Ribbentrop then had to promise to observe the requirements of 'total war' in his own ministry in future.

Despite his self-glorification, Ribbentrop would always accept the advice of one person other than Hitler – his wife. Her influence was at all times so overwhelming that we were not the only ones to make fun of it and discuss the measures introduced by Ribbentrop's 'state secretary'. She even looked over important dispatches, as we heard from Ribbentrop's closest circle. Hitler trusted him, however, and appreciated his readiness to act and his personal courage which – as Hitler assured us – Ribbentrop had proved in the First World

War. He consulted Ribbentrop in all foreign operations but made Ribbentrop read his own foreign policy speeches to him before delivering them in order to avoid any unpleasant surprises.

Hitler's love for architecture and building in general brought him in contact with engineers and architects such as Todt, Speer, Troost and others who were in a position to realise his ideas. Dr Fritz Todt, who built the autobahns and the Westwall defences, and whom Hitler had appointed Minister for Armaments on account of his remarkable talent for organisation, was killed at FHQ Wolfsschanze in February 1942 when his He 111 crashed on take-off. This was a serious loss for Hitler. He suspected that the 'Secret Service' had had a hand in it and ordered a full investigation, which established that the aircraft had just left the ground before crashing and 'disintegrating'. A reconstruction of the machine was not possible, which reinforced Hitler's belief that there had been an explosion using foreign explosives. We were instructed about all kinds of bombs and the places they would be hidden in an aircraft, and from then on before every flight we had to search Hitler's fleet for suspicious packages.

Albert Speer had become a member of Hitler's inner circle before the war. A studio had been placed at his disposal on Obersalzberg so that Hitler could discuss with him his building plans whenever he needed. Speer, a fine-looking, outgoing and very friendly man of aristocratic origins placed no value on outward appearances and military manners and was extremely well-liked by us – and not only because Hitler was fond of him. It spoke for itself that as Reichs Minister for Armaments and Munitions he wore the simple uniform of the lowly Organisation Todt, and this irritated not only the snobs. When I asked him once if he would not prefer to wear a general's uniform as his predecessor had done, he smiled and replied: 'I am not going to make the same error as Todt. He ran around like a general and made himself dependent on the judgement of every military high-up for all important decisions. And I am also not going to click my heels, or say 'Jawohl!'

Hitler valued Speer's sound, practical understanding of people and placed great faith in him. Nevertheless it surprised him that Speer worked his way so quickly into his new sphere of activity. He was soon saying that 'Speer had already eclipsed Todt'. The burgeoning war effort made unprecedented demands on the armaments industry. Hitler's demand to raise the fighting potential despite all setbacks and burdens found in Speer the kind of recipient of orders who would have been very difficult to replace. The leaders of industry were understandably taken aback at the tempo of armaments production and the massive yoking-up of industry for the task, but Speer won them over, which surprised even Hitler. He reflected on this once after Speer had left his presence: 'The industrial magnates may think I am mad. But I feel I am only an intermediary between the front and industry. They must remain flexible to meet the future demands of the front irrespective of whether it is panzers today and anti-tank or flak guns tomorrow. Speer does not have an easy office.' Speer got Hitler to invite industrialists to FHQ from time to time for face-to-face talks once the bombing raids on the Reich took on a more devastating form, and not only the civilian population suffered under them but also the centres of armament production.

In 1943 when the RAF bombed the extraordinarily important Möhne and Eder dams, Hitler was shattered and in despair. He was bitterly reproachful towards Göring, accusing him of having encouraged the enemy to make such attacks. Speer, who had been hurriedly summoned to Hitler because of the precarious situation, promised to have the dams rebuilt immediately. This was done in a relatively short period of time. He was rewarded by Hitler's further confidence in him. Speer could now count on obtaining what others sought in vain. Long thereafter Hitler believed whatever Speer told him or reported. Speer's deputy Saur, on the other hand, ran into doubt and rejection. Hitler looked over his dubious statistics and regarded him with undisguised distrust. 'Do not try to fool me with false figures', he said, 'I rely on this data for the front.'

Towards the end of the war Speer, whom Hitler recognised over the course of time to have a strong independent streak, made no secret of his belief that the war was lost, and he attempted to set out his reasons in memoranda. I would watch Hitler put these to one side unread with the comment: 'Speer just wants to prove to me that the war is lost.' Once Hermann Fegelein, Himmler's liaison officer to Hitler, tried to get me to appropriate one of Speer's memoranda. He and Himmler both thought that Speer wanted to throw in the towel, had gone over to the 'defeatist camp' and was endangering 'victory'. I refused to comply explaining that Hitler had ordered me never to give out any document without his prior authority. Surprisingly Bormann also held back even though Speer was his arch-enemy. Perhaps he was looking ahead and wanted Speer as an ally for the hour that was at hand.

At the end of 1945 when chaos reigned and defeat was at hand, Speer called the Reich Chancellery bunker from Hamburg and asked what Hitler intended. As I was in doubt on the matter I replied that he would remain in Berlin and take the consequences. Speer, clearly nervous and shocked, offered at once to send a couple of Fieseler Storch light aircraft from Hamburg to fly out Hitler and Eva Braun. When I told him there was no point he transferred the call to Eva Braun, but got the same answer from her. This episode made his statement at Nuremberg, that he had considered killing Hitler by poisoning him in the Reich Chancellery bunker, seem absurd.

Hitler met Erich Raeder, Kriegsmarine commander-in-chief until the end of 1942, for the first time just before the seizure of power. He had invited Hitler to inspect warships even before he became Reich Chancellor. On that occasion Hitler had emphasised that the navy, contrary to what was always maintained, had not remained 'imperially minded'. It had interested itself in National Socialism and Hitler, whilst the army had a closed mind for these ideas. Repeatedly Goebbels had been refused permission to address the officer corps on the National Socialist political world-view.

From early on Hitler saw in Raeder a man upon whom he could build. Although it was joked at the time that 'the navy will never be anything while it runs on wheels' (*Raeder* = wheels), for Hitler Erich Raeder was the most able man upon whom he could rest his hopes for his favourite arm of the military. Hitler knew the navy better than any admiral. Experts in naval warfare were not happy with him in question-and-answer sessions at technical conferences. The extent of Hitler's knowledge is shown not least by his designs for new battleships. Because giant battleships offered bombers an easy target, he wanted to do away with the old 'naval review types' as he called them. All superstructure except the bridge would disappear in future, and the upper deck – enclosed within a lateral trench-type arrangement for the crew – was to be heavily armoured. Only the heavy guns would be above deck, the medium and light weapons he would have installed lower down.

During the war he designed a cruiser with a catapult launch for aircraft that could be partially dismantled and stowed below deck. The responsible naval people rejected it on the grounds that the Royal Navy had nothing like it and the type was therefore not 'classic'. One day at lunch a despatch arrived stating that the British were building that very sort of cruiser. With a triumphant smirk Hitler passed the paper to his naval adjutant, Admiral von Puttkamer, with the words: 'The British are now building the cruiser and from now on it will be classic.' Puttkamer was stupefied. What could he say?

Hitler told me that in his youth he had studied naval questions very intensively. Occasionally he would draw warships and ships' gunnery of all kinds. It was a pastime of his. Whether any of it was ever tried out or realised in practice I never discovered. I was never very interested in the Kriegsmarine. I often heard Grossadmiral

Karl Dönitz praise the Führer's detailed knowledge and inventive ability in naval matters. One of these inventions I remember very clearly. It was at the end of October 1941. Hitler had an idea for a 'hybrid' mine-torpedo. The mine would be activated by the noise of a ship's propellers, attracted towards the source magnetically and explode against the ship's hull. If it remained activated, the mine would automatically defuse itself after five years so as not to be a danger to commercial shipping.

On our trips away I always had to bring three naval tomes – *Jane's* (the English-language book of the naval fleets), Weyer's *Flottenkalendar* (the German equivalent) and the current Kriegsmarine yearbook. Hitler knew them almost by heart. During the invasion of Norway the navy was engaged for the first time in a major action. The military men 'had the jitters', but Hitler, though very excited and nervous, tried to give the appearance of calm confidence. 'Even if we lose our surface fleet in order to occupy Norway', he told Keitel and Jodl, 'the navy will have won itself a page of fame in history.' Hitler put an end to an argument, in which the military people had asserted that the German navy only had 'small tubs', by saying that in future he wanted to build only small, very manoeuvrable warships which would offer the enemy a very poor target. When Dönitz once challenged this concept, Hitler asked him: 'What happens when the big ships are sunk? The crew gets into small boats. Why go round in a circle?' This left Dönitz speechless.

The star of Erich Raeder was so much in the ascendant after the successful landings in Norway that Hitler summoned him one day for some 'private' advice. Although much of it was not intended for others to hear, my presence did not appear to concern Hitler. Most noteworthy for me was Hitler's advice to Raeder to drop the 'Dr h.c.' as the prefix to his name. Before the surprised admiral could respond, Hitler asked with a smile: 'How would it have looked,

Herr Generaladmiral, if Otto von Bismarck had had printed on his letterheads 'Dr h.c. Otto von Bismarck'? Raeder looked quite hurt.

In the ten years that I knew him, but especially from 1936, Hitler was constantly worried about his health. From what he told me I knew that since the end of the First World War he had suffered stomach trouble, which he blamed on his irregular lifestyle after his release from the army. This had sapped his strength. Because the problem would not go away he had sought relief in all manner of new medicines. Dr Conti, later Reich Health Minister and Hitler's first 'personal physician', advised him to simply eat what he fancied. This brought no relief from the discomfort. Other doctors were consulted. One of them, surgeon Dr Karl Brandt, stayed with Hitler and became his auxiliary physician, constantly on hand when travelling. Brandt and another surgeon, Professor Haase, were replaced by Dr Hasselbach whenever Hitler was in Bavaria.

One day 'official Reich photographer' Heinrich Hoffmann introduced Hitler to the Berlin specialist for intestinal disorders, Dr Theo Morell. He had a large practice in the capital, where he treated many showbusiness people, businessmen and diplomats. He was considered to have unconventional ideas, but these seemed vindicated by good results. Morell could not placate Hitler's fears about his health, however. He was obsessed by the idea that Hitler's difficulties would cease if he, a total vegetarian, did not have ordinary vegetables and salads, but only those grown under special conditions. In a special vegetable garden the plants would have to be correctly manured in a mixture of soils to be converted into material which in Morell's opinion would not damage Hitler's organism. When the doctors advised Hitler to include at least a little animal fat in his diet he waved the suggestion away. It was not easy for Morell to be Hitler's physician.

Hitler's physical decline began very early on, and nobody recognised this better than himself, but he was deaf to medical advice to change his diet and introduce a normal rhythm to his life. At the end of 1942 when the fighting at Stalingrad reached a threatening stage, his left hand began to tremble. He made a great attempt to suppress this and hide it from outsiders. By pressing the hand against his body, or grasping it firmly with the right, he tried to conceal the condition but found this very difficult to do, especially after similar symptoms began to affect his left leg.

Because the passionate cake-lover Hitler feared getting fat, he kept a strict eye on his weight. Corpulence, he believed, could reduce his standing in the eyes of the public. Therefore he often took strong purges and later opium to settle his stomach, followed by a medicine to kill gastric bacteria. He also resorted to these desperate cures when his stomach trouble was very bad, which he now tended to blame on his internal struggles with the military. Occasionally I helped him in this respect by keeping his medicine chest well stocked so that his requirements could be met on demand. After the assassination attempt of 20 July 1944 there was an improvement for a while, but this proved only a respite. Medicines were then drawn from the Waffen-SS medical office instead of the pharmacy, as he had a fear of being poisoned.

Although he often spoke after 1936 of an early death and asked us to consider life without him, he was never overcome with self-pity. He would only confine himself to bed if he was ill and had no option. He was so good at putting on a show that people who did not know him well would not notice that he was sick. Nobody was to be informed of any of his infirmities. Not even Eva Braun should find out. He would telephone her as usual, omitting to mention that he was speaking to her from his sickbed. Sometimes the stomach gripes caused him to double up when he thought nobody was looking. Not only did he want to appear 'healthy', to be 'present and correct' at all times, but he also bore the pain without complaint even when there was no necessity to do so. Hence the surprise of Dr Erwin Giesing at Hitler's decision not to have anaesthetics for operations.

When Giesing operated on Hitler's ear after the Stauffenberg attempt, Hitler merely requested that I should hold him down. 'What my soldiers have to endure daily at the front I must also be able to tolerate,' he said, and forbade all further discussion about the unnecessary pain.

Chapter 12

Resolving the Polish Question: September 1939

D URING THE WAR HITLER was little more than a warlord, strategist and soldier. He isolated himself from 'the world' beyond policymaking and ignored those matters that until then he had considered his principal preoccupation. He imposed upon himself exaggerated and superfluous obligations and acted as though he were supposed to lead a more modest and blameless life than anybody else. He eschewed the film shows with his intimate circle, the hours with gramophone records, the picnics and other travels cross-country in which he had previously delighted. That he largely withdrew himself from affairs of government was another serious consequence of the war. Whereas up to 1939 he had been constantly involved in all kinds of governmental problems, it was now piecemeal, case to case, and when time allowed that he heard what his ministers, the Reichsleiters, Gauleiters, governor-generals and commissioner-generals had to report on their activities, successes and failures.

The abandonment of the joint discussions between ministers and Gauleiters during the war deprived government of the concerted line of action necessary in many cases. The politicians and civil servants at the highest levels who had responsibility for events discovered later what their opposite numbers had done, which often resulted in their both being beset by problems particularly in those cases where they had made mutually conflicting decisions. Communal decision-making was a thing of the past. Without Bormann there would certainly have been chaos. That despite all these deficiencies Hitler remained the lord of the land and knew almost everything everywhere was one of the reasons why politicians, civil servants and numerous military men were inclined to believe him a genius. If Hitler deliberately cultivated this style of government and leadership to create such an outcome I have no idea. He did say once or twice: 'What would you all do if I were not there?' but that might not necessarily have been in the same context. So far as I could judge the military knew in principle what would have to be done without Hitler, but it would have been chaotic for the civilian population. Bormann had the Party and its leaders in the palm of his hand, but if Hitler no longer existed Bormann, a person whose name was virtually unknown amongst the general population, would have been totally powerless.

It is not for me to attempt judgement on the achievements of the German generals during the war. I could enter the situation conference at any time without being announced if I wanted to see and hear what was going on, but I only did this when I had reason to. Moreover I did not have the factual material to assess the measures imposed, the justification for them and the way they fitted into the overall picture in any particular theatre of war. What is certain, however, is that a great deal of the so-called 'history' that the German generals were pleased to present to the world after 1945 did not happen in the way they sought to describe. Discussions to which I was an 'eyewitness' appeared in a different light to that which I recall. Whilst the situation conferences were recorded by sworn stenographers, this did not usually happen in talks between Hitler and individual military officers, so at times he would be glad to see me in the room as an impartial witness. Thus in certain situations, and this occurred more frequently in the latter half of the war, Hitler would ask, in the presence of a conversation partner or an officer to whom he had given an order in the past: 'Linge, what did I say then, and what did General X suggest?' If additional confirmation were needed by checking the stenographic records, he would send me into the stenographers' room, to which only he, Schaub and myself were allowed access. Many generals, relying on their memory, might have believed that I gave the record a slant, as I never returned with an answer that would have obliged Hitler to correct his previous recollection of the facts. The fact is the stenographic record always confirmed that Hitler said what he insisted he had said. If it had been any different I would certainly have said so.

When war began, Hitler shut a door behind him which he never re-opened. This was shown not only by the stark re-orientation of his activities. In the second half of August 1939, when the telephone lines in Berlin, Munich and Berchtesgaden 'ran hot', and the door catches were virtually untouched, it was absolutely clear to me that, despite many public announcements to the contrary, the good times were at an end. From Hitler himself I learned nothing. His lips were sealed. Even Eva Braun, who on taking her leave of him on 24 August had asked concernedly how long he was thinking of staying in Berlin and when he would return to the Berg, received only the words 'in two or three days' in answer. The comings and goings of politicians and diplomats, whose excitement and tension created a weird atmosphere, gave the lie to his assurance.

On 14 August Hitler received the commanders-in-chief of the three Wehrmacht arms of service and Dr Todt. On 22 August the commanders-in-chief met again together with a number of generals. Next day Ribbentrop flew to Moscow, and on 24 August the public was informed of the signing of the German-Soviet Non-Aggression Pact in Moscow. In Berlin the pace picked up. On 26 August conferences were held from early to late, which did nothing to reduce the excitement. The reason for this I learned in Bormann's office. Hitler had wanted to attack Poland that day, but the British ratification of their treaty with Poland, and the decision of the Italians not to enter the war on Germany's side dissuaded him. 'From 25 August the German mobilisation proceeds in silence,' I read in a note from Bormann which he had passed to one of his advisers, and on 29 August this person told me that from something Bormann had said he understood that the mobilisation was going ahead despite the negotiations and would be complete by 31 August.

Hitler was extremely edgy. He treated the military adjutants Schmundt and Engel like corporals. He griped about the general staff and accused them of being afraid to fight. He, the Führer and supreme commander, did not want their advice. The air was thick. That last day of mobilisation I had a sleepless night while Hitler awoke that morning of 31 August having slept calmly and deeply despite all the excitement. Outwardly he gave the impression that it was just another day, although inwardly he was in turmoil. The diplomatic exchanges and the stubbornness of the British got on his nerves, especially since he had made up his mind long before what he was going to do. He had a bad night on 1 September, which was understandable in view of what he had unleashed that day. When he summoned me and asked if his luggage was fully packed and 'ready to go', his breath was so foul that I considered mentioning it to him, for he had appointments to receive not only the generals but also the Swedish industrialist Birger Dahlerus, who was making a last-ditch effort to stop the war. I did not want to call on the physician to do the job for me, for Hitler's breath was almost constantly foul. My deliberations on how to make Hitler aware of the problem were interrupted by his order that in future I should only bring along his field-grey uniforms. Shortly before ten that morning he drove to the Reich Chancellery, already in field-grey, to speak at the Reichstag session. SA formations and SS had begun lining the streets from Wilhelm-Strasse to the Kroll Opera railings since eight o'clock, but it was hardly necessary, for the crowds were very thin on the ground. There was none of the jubilation to be seen which accompanied the outbreak of war in 1914. There were cheers of course, but these were low-key and very muted in comparison with previous expressions of approval.

At the Reichstag all seats were taken, for although about a hundred deputies were absent, Göring, as Reichtag president, had quickly filled the empty places with 'deputy deputies'. Empty seats on the day war broke out would certainly have annoyed more people than Hitler. His nervousness, which I had noticed when I greeted him that morning, had not dissipated and unusually he lacked composure during his speech, occasionally stumbling over his words and looking uncertain. His decision to start the war had been very difficult for him to take, although as we know today he had done everything he could to engineer it. Undoubtedly he was hoping for the Poles to attack Germany, and thus relieve him of the burden. In his Reichstag speech Hitler said:

> For months we have been suffering beneath the weight of a problem created for us by the *Diktat* of Versailles and which has since become intolerable by its degenerate and unnatural form. Danzig was and is a German city! The Corridor was and is German! As always, I have been trying here to change the intolerable situation through peaceful proposals for its revision . . . All these proposals have been rejected. They make it impossible to resolve. They demand that the situation has to be resolved by the path of peaceful revision – and then refuse to allow peaceful revision! How can they maintain that the party proposing these revisions is acting unlawfully? In conversations with Polish statesmen I have discussed the ideas which you learned from me in my last Reichstag address (of 28 April 1939). Nobody can say that this was an improper procedure or even undue pressure. I had the German proposals put into draft form, and I have to repeat once again that there is nothing more honest and modest than the proposals put forward by myself. And I would like to say to the world now: I was not at all alone in making such proposals! I know perfectly well that I see the situation as do millions of Germans. These proposals have been rejected . . . answered by mobilisation, with increased terror, with heightened pressure on the ethnic

Germans in these regions and with a slow economic, political and, finally in recent weeks, also military and communications action to isolate the Free City of Danzig. More than three weeks ago I informed the Polish ambassador that if Poland sent any more Final Notes to Danzig, if they undertook any more repressive measures against the Germans there, or if they attempted to ruin Danzig economically by the imposition of tariffs, then Germany could no longer stand by inactive. I have left no doubt in this respect that the Germany of today is not to be confused with the Germany which preceded us . . . I have made one last attempt! Although convinced inwardly that the Polish government is not serious about wanting a real understanding, I accepted a proposal by the British government for mediation. They suggested that they would not be handling the negotiations themselves, but guaranteed to restore direct contact between Poland and Germany so that dialogue could be continued. I accepted this proposal! I worked out the basic agenda for the talks . . . and then I sat and waited two whole days with my government to see whether it suited the Polish government to finally decide to send a plenipotentiary or not! As at last evening they had still sent no plenipotentiary, but let us know through their ambassador that at the moment they are considering if and to what extent they are prepared to go along with the British proposal: they would let Britain know.

Gentlemen deputies! If the German Reich and its head of state can be treated in that manner, and the German Reich and its head of state accept it, then the German nation would deserve no more than to step down from the political stage. I have given solemn assurances, and I repeat them, that we have no demands to make of the western states and will never make any. I have given the assurance that the frontier between Germany and France is the definitive one. I have repeatedly offered Britain friendship and, if required, the closest cooperation. But love offered by one side cannot stand if not reciprocated by the other. Germany has no interest in the West, our Westwall is the Reich border for all time. Therefore we have no kind of aim for the future, and the Reich's position will not change. The other European states understand our attitude to some extent. Here I would like above all to thank Italy, which has supported us throughout . . . the neutral states have assured us of their neutrality, just as we have already guaranteed theirs.

Our aims, which I am determined to resolve, are 1. The question of Danzig, 2. The question of the Corridor and 3. to ensure that there is a change in the relationship between Germany and Poland which will guarantee peaceful co-existence. I am determined to keep fighting until either this Polish government becomes inclined to accept this change, or until another Polish government is ready to do so.

Last night for the first time, Polish regular troops fired their arms on our territory. Since 0545 hrs[1] we have been returning fire! From now on bomb will be answered with bomb . . . I shall continue this battle, irrespective of against whom, for as long as is necessary to guarantee the security of the Reich, and its rights . . . If I call upon this Wehrmacht, and if I now demand sacrifices of the German people, and if I demand every sacrifice, then I have the right to do so, for I am precisely as ready personally as I was before to make every personal sacrifice! I demand nothing from any German man which I was not ready to do myself at any time over those four years [of World War One] . . . If during this battle anything happens to me, then my first in succession is Party member Göring. Should anything happen to Party member Göring, then his successor is Party member Hess . . . In the case that Party member Hess does not survive, then by means of an Act the Senate will be called upon to elect the most worthy man, that is to say, the bravest man, from amongst them.

---

1 This should have been 'since 0445 hours'.

One word I have never got to know is: capitulation! If anybody is of the opinion that we are approaching difficult times, I would ask them to reflect on how a king of Prussia, with a laughably small kingdom, once faced one of the greatest-ever coalitions, and after three battles at its conclusion emerged victorious because he had the strong heart of one who believed, the kind of heart we need in these times. I would like to reassure the people: November 1918 will never be repeated in German history![2]

The Führer-train *Amerika* became the FHQ. A few days earlier, Erwin Rommel had been promoted general and took over the protection of FHQ as commandant. On 3 September the train left Berlin for Polzin, went from there next day to Plienitz, and on 5 September to the Gross-Born military camp in Pomerania. This was Hitler's base for his sorties to the frontline until the 8th. Rommel, of whom he thought very highly, was responsible for his security beyond the special train, as when he paid visits to the front. Hitler's *Grossdeutschland* batallion consisted of sixteen officers, ninety-three NCOs and 274 men. Hitler allowed Rommel to attend situation conferences, invited him to dine and gave him information, all of which made him appear especially privileged. He explained to Rommel the theory of cooperation between panzers, assault troops and Stuka dive-bombers and showed him how quick victories would prevent the enemy from seizing the tactical and strategic initiative. I had the impression that Rommel soaked up avidly every word the Führer uttered.

Hitler behaved as though he were on manoeuvres in the field. He went to the front in an armoured car almost daily, passing through woodland and other insecure areas where Polish snipers laid in wait. Once when driving through a wood on the Vistula we came across the bodies of a German medical team massacred twenty

2 DNB Text, 1 September 1939.

minutes before. Hitler, angered, murmured: 'They will have to pay for that!' Even then he showed no fear. He talked to the common infantrymen and told them of his own experiences at the front in the First World War. He enjoyed it when they looked at him with pride, full of hope. In a show of solidarity he ate with the men at the field kitchens and recommended that in future the Gauleiters should follow his example.

During one of our first excursions to the front, one of the generals, apparently disapproving of Hitler's confident outlook, remarked that the campaign was a risky adventure. Giving a stern look, Hitler retorted: 'It is easy for you. We have the adventures behind us.' That evening when I was alone with him, however, he said: 'Everything must keep going fast, as fast as possible. We must bring the enemy to his knees in the quickest time possible. Then nobody else will have the opportunity to call this an adventure.'

He kept himself continually informed of the situation in the West. The fear of war on two fronts preoccupied him more than he cared to admit. Not so Rommel, who was of the opinion on 1 September that the whole thing would be over within fourteen days. When it seemed probable that the British and French were holding back, Hitler confirmed with satisfaction – referring to the Westwall – that his prediction had turned out right. With a sly dig at Hewel, who had believed that if Germany attacked Poland then Britain would join in the land fighting, he said that 'The British and French have had enough of world wars. Whoever thought they were serious about intervening for Poland and keeping to their pact obligations has learnt nothing from history.' Impatient and inwardly tense on 19 September in his HQ at the coastal resort of Zoppot, he waited to enter Danzig, the ostensible reason for the whole affair.

At last, sitting behind him in the car as always, at just after four in the afternoon we entered the city. The indescribable jubilation of the Danzig population made conversation in the open vehicle impossible and quite erased the memory of the arid reception Hitler got in Berlin on 1 September. I had a theatre-box on history, and remained in it until it collapsed six years later.

The welcome for Hitler in Danzig exceeded everything he had ever known previously, including the triumphant entries into Linz and Vienna. Standing up in the car as it rolled forward at a walking pace, he thanked the population which, drunk with joy, bombarded him with bouquets of flowers and posies. I pretended that one of the bouquets had hit me in the face so that people should not know the real cause for the tears in my eyes, although everybody – except Hitler – was fighting back his tears of emotion. Hitler did seem touched by it but was otherwise unperturbed.

In front of the Danzig Artushof, Gauleiter Forster, Danzig NSDAP leaders, Keitel, Rommel, Lammers, Himmler, Dr Dietrich, Bormann and Hitler's adjutants awaited him. In his address he spoke of 'the victorious eighteen-day campaign' despite the fact that Warsaw was still holding out and there was fighting on the Hela Peninsula.

In just eighteen days we have crushed Poland and thus brought about the circumstances which will perhaps make it possible to speak to the representatives of this people reasonably and quietly. Meanwhile Russia also sees the necessity to march into Poland and so protect the interests of the White Russian and Ukrainian elements there. We now discover that Britain and France see in this collaboration between German and Russia a terrible crime, and an Englishman even called it perfidy. The British would know all about that! I believe that the British see as perfidious the failure of their attempt at collaboration between democratic Britain and Bolshevist Russia, while the attempt between National Socialist Germany and Bolshevist Russia succeeded. I would like to make a declaration here: Russia will remain what it is, and Germany will also remain what it is! On one thing, however, both regimes are clear: neither the German nor the Russian regime wishes to sacrifice a single life for the interests of the Western democracies. The lessons of four years of war are enough for both states and both peoples.[3]

Later, when Hitler's sureness had returned and he was in good humour I asked him how he could speak of victory in eighteen days when the situation was otherwise. His explanation was both convincing and plausible. On 17 September 1939, corresponding to the mutual agreement, the Russians invaded a Poland which had already been mortally wounded. For political and propaganda purposes, the Soviets were not to bask in any of the glory of victory. Moreover, as he finished off with a significant smile, he had also said 'clearly': 'Russia will remain what it is and Germany will also remain what it is.'

From the Kasino Hotel at Zoppot where he had set up his HQ, Hitler went to the Hela Peninsula where the Poles were still offering stiff resistance at the beginning of October. What interested him here most of all was the effect that our naval gunnery and Stuka bombing had had. I had the sensation of going through a wood in which the trees had been felled. That the greater part of our cities and much of Europe would look the same a few years later, and that this war would last six years as the Second World War, and cost 40 million people their lives, I could not anticipate. At that time the very idea would have appeared absurd to me. We had incorporated into the Reich the Saarland, Memel, the Sudetenland and Austria without serious opposition and had now put down Poland in less than three weeks while its allies, Britain and France, stood by as if paralysed. Even if things turned out unexpectedly, I was totally convinced by Hitler's successes to date that the last batallion on the battlefield would be a German one.

---

3 DNB Text, 19 September 1939.

When we drove to Gotenhafen (Gdynia), the city that the Poles had defended longest, there was a domestic incident. Bormann and Rommel were massing their respective groups. Hitler, for whom everything was moving too slowly, ordered our driver to go down a narrow and fairly steep road to the harbour. This created a problem in that the car carrying the SS bodyguard had to stick to our tail. Rommel, knowing this, positioned himself on the street and roared like a sergeant: 'Only the Führer and the bodyguard's motors are to go down! All others wait here!' As we started up and I looked behind me, I saw a third car in motion. This vehicle contained Bormann, who was gesticulating wildly at Rommel. I knew them both as stubborn and ambitious thickheads obsessed with power. They ought never to have squared up to each other like this, but here they were, both at it right behind Hitler's back. Bormann got his version in first. Rommel had blocked his path and had declared brusquely and 'disrespectfully': 'Remain where you are. I order it as the FHQ commandant. This here is no kindergarten outing. Kindly do as I have ordered!' To Bormann's chagrin Hitler merely responded: 'No, a kindergarten outing it certainly is not!' Accustomed as I was to Bormann's peculiarities and love of intrigue, the ugly thought assailed me that Bormann would seek his revenge. Five years later, almost to the day, he got it. Rommel's suicide was decided at his desk.

Rommel's intrepid ways and Hitler's admiration of him left scars not only on Bormann. Oberst Rudolf Schmundt, the senior military adjutant, felt snubbed and showed it relatively often. He also said so to Hitler. The latter evidently foresaw great things for the general from Ulm who wore the Pour le Mérite awarded him in the First World War. Scarcely had Warsaw fallen than Hitler gave Rommel the order to prepare the victory parade for 5 October 1939, a task any general would dream of. It was a gloriously sunny day. Rommel stood immediately before Hitler's podium. This placed him at the immediate forefront of all the world's press and newsreel reports on Hitler's great triumph.

Behind the scenes, in Hitler's closest circle, it was clear that there was water in the wine. Dr Karl Brandt, Hitler's travelling physician, had returned the day before from Münster, where he had had a general discussion on the Jewish question with Cardinal Clemens August Graf von Galen. They also talked about public opinion on the war and the general mood amongst the German people. Brandt, hanged by the Americans at Landsberg Prison after being found guilty of crimes against humanity at Nuremberg, came back from Münster depressed. At the beginning of the war he had been given the job of organising the euthanasia programme, the destruction of 'worthless lives', and the cardinal had impressed him deeply, something he made no attempt to conceal. 'My God', he said, 'if I told the Führer everything the cardinal said to me, the cardinal and I would both be in a concentration camp by morning.'

Although I believed firmly in the rightness of the Führer's decisions, I now had my first doubts, for as I always confirmed of him, Karl Brandt was a skilful and responsible doctor who was first and foremost a healer and not a 'Nazi'. He was neither a career man, nor one of those who 'wanted to be something' at any price, but a medical practitioner in whom everybody could place his or her confidence. How often I now saw him, a man outwardly so heroic and soldierly, depressed and reflective. How often he said to me contritely: 'Linge, the Führer is surrounding himself with the wrong people, but keep that to yourself.' As I saw nearly every day the friction between him and Hitler's personal physician Morell, who was senior to him, and knew that his remarks did not arise from envy for Morell's position, I did not consider them important enough for me to have report them to Hitler. Brandt, who joined the SS as an Unterscharführer on 29 July 1934 and by April 1944 had reached the rank of SS-Gruppenführer, had been responsible for the euthanasia programme from 1 September 1939. He never spoke of it to Hitler, and in public used to make statements that he was satisfied and even 'inspired'. How should I have 'got involved'? The fact that I was less well educated than surgeon Brandt, who was therefore better able to judge and had better insight about people than I did, relieved me of the burden of this decision to the extent that I could view the spontaneous expressions of doubt which Brandt had communicated to me in another light. Unlike Brandt, I was not in a position to pretend, like some skilled actor, that things were just wonderful. Mostly, when asked by ministers and Gauleiters exuding confidence on a visit to see Hitler, how I 'standing constantly at three steps behind or to the side of the Führer' could wear 'such a sour face' when everything 'was going so well', I just gave a shrug. I was not only deeply influenced by Hitler but was also sworn to total, uncritical obedience to him. I could only reason with myself: my position does not allow my personal doubts to affect my composure. And that was how I left it to the bitter end. I could not under any circumstances permit my actions to deviate from any decision made by Hitler, a man to whom I was specially bound as his subordinate, having sworn an oath to sacrifice my life for him at any time and under any conditions should the occasion require me so to do.

Chapter 13

The Phoney War

ON 26 SEPTEMBER 1939, 'the war now being at an end', we returned to Berlin aboard the Führer-train. Next day at Wilhelmshaven Hitler conferred with von Brauchitsch, Halder, Dönitz and a number of other military men. After that we remained until 19 December (with short breaks on 7, 8, 11, 24, 25 and 26 November) in the Reich capital, where Hitler was confronted by influential military men bearing reports that left him disappointed and enraged. Especially the army commander-in-chief von Brauchitsch talked about the army disintegrating, of mutinies, illegal shootings and acts of sabotage in Poland, all of which proved to be hugely exaggerated. Hitler was not altogether happy with his victory. He criticised 'the gentlemen of the army' and made no secret of his 'justifiable sympathy for the SS', as he put it. I was hoping more fervently at this time than during the 'eighteen days of September' that it was the last we would have of war. I saw how Hitler was plagued by doubt, how suspicious he was of the army generals, how the flame of this suspicion repeatedly flared and how he tried to keep all this a secret.

If free expression had not been suppressed so ruthlessly, if details had become known to the fighting units, to the enemy and amongst the population at large, Hitler would have found it very difficult to have gone on with the war. The Elser assassination attempt of 8 November 1939 at the Bürgerbräukeller in Munich, the act of a lone individual, could be seen as an expression of a section of public opinion. Precisely for that reason neither Hitler nor Himmler wanted to believe that Elser had nobody behind him, someone for whom he was only the tool.

Sharing Hitler's disappointment with events was a young Englishwoman in a Munich clinic. Unity Mitford* had shot herself in the head the day Britain declared war on the Reich. Although seriously wounded, she had survived. Hitler, who had received her regularly before the war, had gone to her bedside to comfort her on 8 November, a few hours before his speech at the Bürgerbräukeller, and immediately afterwards had ordered arrangements to be made for her repatriation to England via Switzerland. As sorry as he felt for the pretty and charming blonde who adored him, now he had to be uncompromising. 'It is war', he said, 'everything else must take a back seat.'

One month later on 6 December 1939 Hitler visited Feldmarschall von Mackensen to offer his congratulations on his ninetieth birthday and present him with a valuable painting of an equestrian scene. He very much looked forward to meeting the aged celebrity, whom he knew to be one of his fervid supporters. Mackensen came to attention to greet the supreme warlord, then showed him his many presents, amongst them a portrait of Kaiser Wilhelm II with a personal dedication. The old general had prepared for the Führer's visit as though it were a military parade. If I remember correctly he had even used a bit of make-up. He discussed with Hitler the Polish campaign and the old army, and with a wavering voice and tears in his eyes proclaimed: 'My great Führer, if I were a few years younger I would be at your disposal.' Hitler was recharged with confidence and energy. The escort and Mackensen's guests were then treated to a captivating cameo: the legendary old figure bowing to fifty-

---

* Unity Valkyrie Mitford (b. 8.8.1914 London). On 3 September 1939 in the Englischer Garten (near Königin-Strasse 15) she shot herself in the head. Repatriated to England through Switzerland on Hitler's instructions, she died on 20 May 1948. (TN)

year-old Hitler, addressing him as 'my great Führer', predicting that Hitler would lead the German Wehrmacht to fame and glory and declaring in excited, trembling tones: 'My great Führer, do not worry about the unimportant things such as Holland and Belgium. These must be overrun.' As we drove back, Hitler reflected: 'Pity he is too old. Now there is a model for our weakly and anxious military.' Mackensen was a man to his taste.

At the time of the Polish campaign Hitler would occasionally remark that during his excursions across the country his impressions convinced him that he ought to resolve the Jewish question in Poland as soon as possible, now that it was a region of German influence. Although the Polish Jews exercised no great influence on Polish politics, it seemed to him necessary to take the same steps as in the Reich after the passing of the Nuremberg Laws. The ghettoes at Lublin and Lodz then in preparation would not be sufficient for the purpose. Up to this point Hitler had apparently not planned anything, possibly not even given it a thought, for in his conversations with Arthur Greiser, Deputy Gauleiter of Danzig, and Gauleiter Albert Forster, neither of them had brought up the subject with him. He did think that the man from Franconia in western Germany, Forster, was weak in comparison to Greiser: Forster did not know the Poles and was promulgating an 'army proposal about a possible moderate Poland-policy' while Hitler was relying on Greiser, and particularly Himmler, to start the ball rolling by installing a very harsh and rigorous police chief in Danzig. Once when Baldur von Schirach, Hermann Esser, Dr Dietrich, the Munich Gauleiter Adolf Wagner and Wilhelm Murr, Gauleiter and Reich governor of Württemberg were his guests, Hitler recalled how in 1937 he had offered to sell the 600,000 German Jews to Britain as a workforce for Palestine. This had seemed a good way to clear the Jews out of the Reich and do a deal with London, but in the upshot, as he said with a laugh, 'our cousins over there did not welcome the idea'. They did not want the German Jews. There was general laughter when he mentioned an observation by Stalin in this connection that, during the negotiations on their respective zones of influence, Ribbentrop had diplomatically and in a very refined manner rejected the Suvalki region as a border for East Prussia because 'there were an awful lot of Jews there' and he was 'quite sure that the Führer would not like it'.

Because biological anti-Jewry was inbred into National Socialism, which every German must have experienced in some way or another between 1933 and 1939 without even reading *Mein Kampf* or *Der Stürmer*, Hitler's statements in that respect never raised an eyebrow with us. On the contrary. Despite my proximity to Hitler, I knew as little about Himmler's special plenipotentiary powers as did the generals – Hitler's ability to keep a secret was unparalleled. Nobody found out more than it was absolutely necessary for him to know in a given situation, and nobody was excluded from this rule, neither Bormann, Himmler, Göring nor Eva Braun. Perhaps this was possible because Hitler had no real friend in the traditional sense of the word.

Hitler's extreme dissatisfaction with a section of the military led him to consider for a while finding a role for the First World War veteran Ludendorff, who had marched with him on 9 November 1923 to the Feldherrnhalle and been acquitted later in the joint Hitler–Ludendorff treason trial. He visited the argumentative general and explained his plans. He was unsuccessful. Mathilde Ludendorff was entrenched against Hitler, and so General Ludendorff had to decline. Hitler raged against his 'Canossa gang' as he called it. Thinking it over he added: 'I should have remembered something Dietrich Eckart said before I went there the first time.' Apparently Eckart had told him in 1923, pointing to Ludendorff: 'Adolf, no genius looks like that.' His search for geniuses continued, and even more so for impetuous followers in a general's uniform.

Quarrels with von Brauchitsch, the army commander-in-chief, of whom Hitler had wished to be rid at the beginning of November, reinforced his opinion that the military understood nothing of politics and did not want war. He would really like 'to smoke out the entire general staff', he said. The population, he remarked in annoyance, thought the German army was the Salvation Army, and neither the population at large nor the enemy suspected how difficult it was 'to fight this war with these people'. The army generals reacted with consternation upon discovering in the last week of November 1939 that nothing would come of the hoped-for separate peace treaty with a Polish government and that the French were resolute on attacking in the West before Christmas. He did not want to wait, he observed mordantly, until the defeatism of the generals had infected the men. Spending long periods of idleness, he went on, made the troops tired of war as they preferred to have fun. Hints about difficulties caused by the climate in winter he dismissed by arguing that 'technology defeats winter'.

At this time Hitler was wracking his brain for a successor to von Brauchitsch. The names of Eugen von Schobert, Heinz Guderian and Walter von Reichenau came up but none suited Hitler, and now he was even more upset after the *SS-Polizei* Division (formed in 1939 and transferred into the Waffen-SS in February 1942) expressed a wish for divisional priests. 'Divisional priests', he said, 'would be more use as divisional drivers'. All Hitler needed now was for the SS to want priests. Bormann seized the opportunity to propose that the singing of hymns should be outlawed in the Wehrmacht if the Führer was present. Since Christmas was coming, Hitler delivered a monologue on Christmas and Christmas carols which, unlike Bormann, he considered beautiful and uplifting. Bormann had to stand by and listen to himself being called a philistine who did not understand what he was saying. 'What more beautiful sound could there be', Hitler asked, 'than *Silent Night, Holy Night?*' Anybody who wanted to ban that sinned against culture. Shame on him. Bormann was visibly hurt. His shocked expression betrayed clearly his upset at having put his foot in it so badly.

Christmas came and went without the campaign in the West having commenced.[1] On 23 December 1939 Hitler travelled to the Limburg aerodrome and Montabaur to visit the *Grossdeutschland* regiment and the *SS-Leibstandarte*, and this meant I missed out on Christmas with my family. On Christmas Eve we celebrated with troops in the Saarbrücken area and went next day to Speyerdorf and Steinheim to call on Infantry Regiment List. We returned to Berlin on Boxing Day and went to Munich from there on 30 December. New Year's Eve saw us at Berchtesgaden, where Hitler celebrated the New Year with Eva Braun.

On 1 March 1940 the US Under-Secretary of State Sumner Welles appeared. He had been in Rome, and after talks with the French and Ribbentrop he was going on to Paris and London, and from there back to Rome to discuss with the respective statesmen 'the possibility for a lasting and secure peace in Europe'. Welles's visit annoyed Hitler, who saw it as an undisguised attempt by US President Roosevelt to pre-empt him, the Führer. Nevertheless he received Welles on 2 March in Berlin in the presence of Otto Meissner, Ribbentrop and the US commercial attaché Alexander Kirk.

After Welles had left the Reich Chancellery, Hitler behaved as though he had won some kind of victory and remarked to his tea circle that he 'had let him have it'. According to Meissner, Hitler had been 'in top form'. The main point he made clear to the American was that Germany had not declared war on Britain and France; Britain and France had declared war on Germany, and thus they were responsible for the current state of affairs. Welles should inform his president that Hitler's aim, and that of the Reich, was peace. Sumner Welles, who had started off by emphasising that he had no authority to make any proposals or binding agreements in the name of the United States, had been very impressed by the Führer's explanation and thanked him for 'the open and frank way' in which

---

1 The attack in the West was originally set for 12 November 1939.

Hitler had spoken to him.[2] Hitler, who had forbidden the army to meet 'the cunning fox' Welles, was convinced that the American understood that he would brook no interference in his policies and would do whatever he thought was right after the West had rejected his proposals for a 'peaceful' accord. The previous day, 1 March 1940, when Welles was speaking to Ribbentrop, Hitler had been signing the order for Operation *Weserübung*, the occupation of Norway and Denmark.[3] He had been doing what he thought was right, as he had assured the US Under-Secretary of State.

Raeder had informed Hitler as to the negative consequences should the British occupy Norway first, and advised him shortly afterwards that such an invasion was being planned in London. Hitler pondered on this a great deal. To lose the Norwegian iron-ore traffic would hit German war industry hard. Hitler therefore decided that he had to pre-empt the British at the last moment. When their ships were ready to sail, the Kriegsmarine was already off the Norwegian ports on 9 April. Beforehand there had been talks in the Old Reich Chancellery. Hitler had told General von Falkenhorst to draw up the invasion plans as quickly as possible. To set the date for the landings a meteorologist was brought in to prepare a weather forecast for the Scandinavian area without letting him know what particular region they were interested in. Hitler was very tense. 'Norway must never become Britain's aircraft carrier,' he said. Repeatedly he left the conference room and went to his study to eat sweets. When I asked him if he were hungry, he replied: 'For me, sweets are the best food for the nerves.' Now that he was placed on the spot to name the date for the attack he felt unwell. The circumstances, that is to say, the threatened British invasion of Norway, forced him – the man who liked to postpone these big decisions – to act. And he had to act now

---

2 For Hitler's talk with Sumner Welles, see Andreas Hillgruber, *Staatsmänner und Diplomaten bei Hitler*, Frankfurt/Main 1967, pp.68ff.

3 The text for the order can be found in Walter Hubatsch (ed.), *Hitlers Weisungen für die Kriegsführung*, Frankfurt/Main 1965, pp.54ff.

if he did not want to get there too late. When the German invasion force was at sea with its occupation troops embarked, the news came that the Royal Navy was also heading for Norway.

Hitler was beside himself with anxiety and feared a major sea battle. Only minor skirmishes occurred. The British Fleet reversed their course. Hitler, who seemed to be relying heavily on Alfred Jodl's support in this situation, was lucky again. I had never seen him so downcast before: now he was visibly relieved and after receiving the message said: 'Luck is with us. Rapid decisions surprise the enemy and usually guarantee success.' When the smaller British ships landed troops in the fjords later, they were overwhelmed by German forces. In the British soldiers' packs, rules of engagement were found which set down with pedantic thoroughness virtually every step to be taken once ashore. Hitler had quickly regained his composure and read through the British instructions, commenting with amusement that the British thought it was 'a sporting event they were coming to' so much sports equipment had they brought along in their packs. That this had not been their intention we were soon to discover.

There was bitter fighting at Narvik. Our troops under Eduard Dietl, who considered Norway to be 'the arse of the world', were so forced into a corner that Hitler considered having them 'escape' through Sweden. That line of thinking was not possible with him later. In this phase of the war it was not Hitler who insisted on 'holding the ground' but the military, particularly Jodl. Although Hitler made every effort to hide from the army this 'fit of weakness', as he later called it, he confessed it freely and without any excuses when he was alone with me. I did not represent 'the opposition' for him, and his admissions of his own defects and weaknesses did not amount to another weakness – on the contrary. Thus as the war dragged on I sometimes played the role of confessor, though all I was required to do was listen.

Chapter 14

The Invasion in the West 1940

I N EARLY MAY 1940 I received orders from Hitler to prepare our belongings for a long journey beginning on the ninth of the month. I was to have them constantly at readiness. After he gave the signal, we left aboard the special train at 1638 hours on 9 May towards Hamburg, which surprised me. Apart from the military adjutants, Hitler had told nobody of the purpose and destination of the journey. It was from them that I found out where we were heading as the result of a basically minor incident. During the journey I ascertained that one of Hitler's trunks had been left behind. My intention was to have it brought up by plane or one of the cars in the entourage. I wanted to arrange this by phone, but the military adjutants refused to let me make the call on secrecy grounds, something that had never happened before. Thus it was easy to draw the conclusion that Hitler was on his way to overwhelm the inconsequential nations of whom von Mackensen had spoken on his ninetieth birthday. The feint northwards was dropped about halfway to Hamburg when the train was rerouted to the west and headed via Uelzen and Celle to Münster in the Eiffel, where we arrived at 0425 hours on 10 May. We continued in a column of vehicles to the village of Rodert near Münstereifel, where FHQ Felsennest was perched on a hill of that name. A gallery had been burrowed into the hilltop to accommodate Hitler's bunker. Everything was rural and primitive. Near Hitler's small bedroom was a workroom containing embrasures. A 'box' about the size of a railway compartment was provided for me. The same was made available for Generaloberst Keitel, near Hitler.

Close to the 'Feldherrnhügel', as we called the bunker hill, there was a small officers' mess where Hitler took meals with his officers until the beginning of June. His mood reflected the weather, pure sunshine. The uncertainty that had dogged him before the Polish and during the Norwegian campaigns was absent. His luck in these operations, almost suspiciously favourable, had made him feel secure. He acted as though this were going to be another 'war followed by bouquets of roses'. When the first Luftwaffe squadron roared away over head, Hitler beamed. His eyes were alight as he watched their flight into the distance, and he gave a smile of contentment.

Every morning he attended the situation conference in a wooden barrack hut some distance away, which housed Jodl and his staff. On the way there – passing through wooded country – he reminded me of a Sunday rambler, admiring Nature, convalescing from his work. He drew my attention to the birdsong and instructed me on the various species. Whoever behaves like this, I told myself, knows exactly what he is doing. It seemed to me that even the doubting military men had less worry lines. Repeatedly they shook their heads in surprise as successes and victories were reported. Hitler was visibly enjoying himself. At the situation conferences where he received the reports and always had an opinion, von Brauchitsch and the chief of the general staff, Halder, principally made the reports. Hitler looked on, and only intervened where the military commanders had conflicting plans or there were political matters to be considered. After these conferences he would go to the officers' mess and mark the new frontline on a large map, indicating the German advance with thick arrows.

On 17 June 1940, via Madrid, the French asked for an armistice. The sceptics were speechless. France, The Netherlands, Belgium and Luxemburg had all fallen. Exactly a month previously he had made his first flight 'to the West' and called on Gerd von Rundstedt at

Bastogne. Twelve days later we retraced his military past in Belgium and France. On 29 May, 2 June, 25 and 26 June we drove to some of the places where he had been a soldier in the First World War. On 29 May we came to a place called Ardooie in Belgian Flanders. He had invited Ernst Schmidt and Max Amann, two of his First World War comrades, on this excursion. Men, women and children lined the kerbside, some smiling and waving, shouting 'Heil Hitler!'. Garlands had been hung in the village, the houses adorned with blooms. Hitler's picture was placed in shop windows. I was surprised at this unusual reception. Hitler was welcomed here as an 'old acquaintance', somebody who 'still belongs here'. He stopped at the old church he had sketched and painted in 1916 and 1917, as he reminded his two companions. One sketch had survived to be reproduced by Heinrich Hoffmann using photographic techniques. Curious inhabitants surrounded our convoy of automobiles as Hitler alighted, looked around and headed for the house of farmer Joseph Goethals at Markt 18, where he had been billeted twenty-three years before. He was met at the gate by his former host and wife. What they spoke about none of us could understand. In any case Hitler, who did not require an interpreter, returned very pensive.

Despite all his triumphs in this era, whatever it was that made him so unusually sentimental, reflective and mild I could never discover. Either he remained silent and meditative, or praised Napoleon and some of the French kings, something I had never heard from him before. He did not mention the black French, of whom he had often spoken previously. His attitude after talks with Fedor von Bock, Küchler and von Reichenau on 1 June in Brussels was also different, although the underlying antipathy remained.

As at Ardooie he reacted similarly at Fournes, Wavrin and Noÿelles-lez-Seclin, places to which he paid special attention. At Fournes, where during the First World War he had had quarters at a butcher's, he even went with Amann and Schmidt to the very room where he slept as regimental despatch runner. Although it struck me that in his conversations with foreigners – contrary to his usual practice – he did not use an interpreter and conducted himself differently, I gave this no more thought. I assumed that the successful warlord had grown sentimental after seeing the old places of his mundane military past. Since there had been no great changes in the region, he remembered every house and farm and even, as at Noÿelles-lez-Seclin, individual trees and railway lines. He had sketched and painted them back then. 'I sat and painted right there', he said at Ardooie, 'and from here I went with Wiedemann and the regimental commander hunting hares at Wavrin.'

On 19 July 1940, about three weeks after our visit to Fournes, we returned to Berlin where he promoted twelve generals, including Keitel, to Generalfeldmarschall. Then Hitler spoke again about the villages and the times he had spent in them in the First World War as a soldier. On this occasion he did not mention the war, fighting and the enemy. Something else was moving him. In general in the weeks up to the middle of August 1940 I had the impression that there had been a 'reconciliation' with the army. What he said was that he had learned from history and promoted those military commanders who had merited it in order to bind them to him. His private mood did not make this very credible, however. Although he was speaking within his close circle of a future attack on Britain and the Soviet Union, we did not take it at face value at the time. Once the order for a general ceasefire (*Das Ganze Halt*) was given at 1335 hours on 24 June 1940, two days before his trip to Fromelles, Fournes, Wavrin and Noÿelles-lez-Seclin, it seemed to us, when we were alone with him, that he had lost some of his belligerency. On 19 July, however, he let the cat out of the bag. He called Himmler and ordered him to look for somebody in the neighbourhood of the village he had mentioned. As Hitler wanted to speak to Himmler alone, and army ADC Gerhard Engel and I quickly left the room, I did not know what detailed instructions Himmler received. Whoever the subject was I did not discover, but there was some talk of a woman and son.

Because Hitler wanted there to be no witness to this conversation with Himmler, I concluded that it really had to be something out of the ordinary. Thirty-seven years later I found out for whom he had been searching: Charlotte Lobjoie, a woman who had born him a son, Jean Marie, in March 1918.[1]

Two days after the Ardooie trip the Italian ambassador, Dino Alfieri, brought Hitler a letter from Mussolini informing him that Italy now desired an active role in the war. Hitler, more surprised than pleased, reacted with sarcasm. 'Now when they see the flock swimming off', he said, 'there is haste to fleece it. My recommendation to the Duce not to enter the war until Italy was ready for it and the moment was opportune seems to have been bad counsel.' In March he had told Mussolini that although he understood Italy's stance in the autumn of 1939, that the Italian army lacked equipment to go to war, he would welcome Italy's entry into the war especially since he had been convinced in 1939 that, if Italy provided Britain and France with a demonstration of readiness to fight alongside Germany, there would have been no declaration of war. Now, when 'everything was over and done with' and the Reich need fear no further danger in the West, Mussolini did what he had been recommended to do at a time when he had not been sure how things would turn out for the Reich. The Italian decision was embarrassing and made it seem that Mussolini was coming along for the ride now that it did not look too dangerous.

Hitler felt very uneasy about it. He criticised the Italian attitude since the outbreak of war and concluded that he was personally in an awkward spot as regards Mussolini. He could hardly forbid the Duce out of hand to stay out of the war. Moreover he had never been really straight with him. In March 1940 when he met Mussolini at the Brenner Pass, he had not told him of his plan to invade Norway since Mussolini did not need to know. Hitler explained: 'If I tell the

---

1 See Werner Maser, 'Adolf Hitler, Vater eines Sohnes' in *Zeitgeschichte*, Hist. Inst. Univ. Salzburg, year 5, February 1978, pp.173ff.

Italians something confidential, next day the world knows. Ciano and the royal house make sure of it.' Nevertheless he told Mussolini of his plan for the West and confided that he was hoping to have defeated France by the autumn of 1940 and to make Britain ready for an 'understanding'. Now he tried to bring Mussolini round. The timing of the Italian declaration of war, as he tried to convince the Duce, was not favourable. It would be best to wait until the Luftwaffe had wiped out the aerodromes in southern France and eliminated any threat to Italy from them.

Mussolini could not step back, however, for the Italian king had already signed the document. Hitler assumed from this that the Italians must have some major operation up their sleeves. 'They will probably blockade Gibraltar and turn the Mediterranean into a witch's cauldron', he told me. 'No British ship will escape the trap. If they do not do that, then they will occupy Malta to bring the Mediterranean Sea under their control.' To Hitler's exasperation, between 10 June 1940 when Italy declared war on Britain and France, and 13 June, when German troops occupied Paris, the Italian operation was revealed at last. Their plan was to do nothing.

In disappointment Hitler wondered if there had been collaboration between the Italian and British royal houses. The Italian royal house, he said tartly, had given the British royal house to understand that Italy would not become involved in the war, and only then did the British make known openly that they would abide by their pact with Poland. He was so angry at this that he made Alfieri come to Bad Godesberg instead of FHQ. All nameplates on his route had to be taken down to prevent him knowing where FHQ Felsennest was located. After Alfieri had left, Hitler was visibly distraught. As always in moments of great tension, he moved his upper body back and forth, contorted his face and ground his jawbone. 'These Italians, these windbags, still do not understand how you start a war in modern times. Nowadays after the declaration of war you have to open fire. When I shouted at Alfieri that nothing had happened after several days had passed, he said the reason was that it was raining on the border with France.' Hitler ridiculed the Italian king, who had made the declaration of war conditional on the crown prince having command of the army. Even though Hitler, as he was fond of pointing out, was convinced that Mussolini knew nothing about warfare, the intention of the Italian king to distance the Duce from the military leadership annoyed him.

On 6 June the FHQ was transferred to a spot near the Belgian/Luxemburg border. In a wood at Brûly-de-Pesche two barrack huts had been put up. One of these was for Hitler, the other served as the officers' mess. The bunker was not habitable because the curing process had overheated the rooms. The staff were lodged in a school in the village and the rectory. Eight days later Paris fell, and on 17 June France sued for peace. I never saw Hitler so happy as he was on that day. Overjoyed he slapped his thigh and did a little dance. The news of the German victory could not be got out fast enough. Next day, 18 June, he met Mussolini in Munich and told him that the most important thing to be done now that the military campaign against France was over was to install a French government on French territory as a negotiating partner. To block off outside influences it was necessary to occupy and secure the entire Channel and Biscay coasts and the harbours of Cherbourg, Nantes and Bordeaux.[2]

During the return journey Hitler praised the insight of the Duce who had suggested amongst other things securing the Paris–Chambery–Bourg–Modane railway line for transports to Italy by the new French government. In the hope of a 'wink and a nod' from the British, to whom he had officially extended peace feelers through the Spanish government, Hitler drafted the armistice conditions and preamble and waited for London to agree to an 'understanding' on the basis of 'dividing up the world'.

---

2 For the conversation between Hitler and Mussolini of 18 June 1940, see Andreas Hillgruber, *Staatsmänner und Diplomaten bei Hitler*, Frankfurt/Main 1967, pp.139ff.

On 21 June 1940, a wonderfully sunny day, we flew to Amiens and drove from there to Compiègne. In the woods at this location where, in Hitler's words, the shame of 1918 would be erased and the honour of the German people restored, he inspected the front rank of each honour company of the three Wehrmacht branches of service paraded for him, then went to a clearing to view the monument erected in 1918 dedicated to the collapse of Germany. Passing the statue of Marshal Foch, he glanced at the marker stone sunk into the ground and ordered it to be blown up.

After that he inspected the railway dining car in which the surrender negotiations between the German and French delegations had been held in 1918, and ordered that the coach should be removed to a historical museum in Berlin. With Hess, Göring, Raeder, von Brauchitsch and von Ribbentrop he occupied one side of the prepared negotiating table in the dining car. I stood at the entrance to the car as the French delegation arrived, led by the small thin General Hunzinger. The honour companies came to attention but did not present arms. When the French delegation entered the car, Hitler and his colleagues rose without speaking. After bowing to each other the delegations resumed their seats. Keitel then read out the preamble to the armistice conditions as Hitler left the wagon, saluting the French delegation as they rose. I gave the honour company a signal, commands were barked out and at once the band struck up 'Deutschland über alles'. Hitler left the wood and returned to FHQ. He who had enjoyed the hour of satisfaction had set out the procedure in detail himself. He wanted to bring home to the French by his haughty demeanour the humiliation which in his view they had made him and the German people suffer in 1918. At FHQ he waited nervously for news of the signing. After a brief wait, in impatience he rang Keitel, who was handling the negotiations at Compiègne. He spoke to Hitler from a tent. The French delegation had conferred with their government by telephone, and after a few discussions declared their readiness to accept the conditions.

Goebbels received instructions from Hitler the same evening to mark the German victory by pealing church bells and general celebrations. Amidst his closest circle in the officers' mess, Hitler heard the radio proclamation to all Germany. As the national anthem was played he rose. We looked at him in silence. After an hour of rest he had the champagne served and we all touched glasses to 'the victory of German arms'.

After long day trips to Laon, Lille, Messines, Fromelles, Fournes etc., on 27 June 1940 the FHQ was transferred to swampy land at 1,000 metres altitude on the Kniebis mountain near Freudenstadt in the Black Forest, where damp and poorly soundproofed subterranean bunkers awaited us. Hitler and I inhabited one of these inhospitable units alone. Until then I had 'lived' in Hitler's immediate presence, but there had always been some other person around, even if it was only Eva Braun. Now I was his only conversational partner when I was in the bunker.

He had been very pleased with our Paris visit of 23 June to the great Opera House. He knew it so well from his book studies that he could act as the 'tourist guide' and astonished everybody, including the Paris experts Speer, Arno Breker and Hermann Giesler, with his detailed and comprehensive knowledge. That Hitler concentrated particularly on Napoleon at this time was not only due to his having visited the sarcophagus of the French emperor during a round of the crypt at the Invalides Cathedral. Since then Hitler had been thinking, he remembered during one such conversation, that he wanted to be interred in the Temple of the Eternal Watch at the Munich Feldherrnhalle. For that purpose, and he actually made arrangements for it in his Will of 2 May 1938, I was to receive a bequest of 3,000 RM in the event of his death with which I had to have a coffin made similar to those of the *Alte Kämpfer* who had 'fallen for the Movement' at the Feldherrnhalle on 9 November 1923. The visit to Napoleon's sarcophagus had helped make him more than a little morbid, and had moved him – though 'only fifty-one year old' – to award Hermann Giesler the job of designing his sarcophagus.

Despite these considerations, accompanied by gloomy thoughts of death, Hitler was in very good spirits at this time. He received visitors, was companionable, invited Black Forest girls for coffee and conversed happily with them. If we had not had to live in the awful bunkers we would have felt like holidaymakers on summer vacation. One day – news had got around that Hitler was there – a beautiful Black Forest girl appeared with a strawberry cake which she handed to Hitler and received in return an invitation from him for coffee. On taking her leave she extended an invitation to a number of men from Hitler's closest circle and myself to her parents' house. The result was a merry gathering which did not end until five next morning. At the midday meal, attended by a host of military commanders and other influential guests, Hitler ordered me to find out at once who had been on watch outside our bunker at five in the early hours. The sentry had 'made such a racket' that it had woken him up and he had not been able to get back to sleep. I was horrified, for I had been the culprit. Braced for an outburst I confessed: 'It was I, mein Führer, but I removed my boots so as not to disturb you.' Instead of the bawling-out I was expecting, Hitler turned to his guests laughing and said: 'There you are, gentlemen. Before you stands a typical married man. Comes home late and creeps to bed in his socks.'

From the way I see it, an anecdote from a few months before Hitler's suicide may provide an alternative assessment of his personality to the 'carpet biter' and hysterical psychopath often portrayed in the literature. A member of the SS bodyguard had to ring the squad paymaster. At the same time Hitler wanted to phone Speer. The SS man was to take his call in a cabin at the officers' mess. Hitler waited for his connection to Speer in the barrack hut for situation conferences. The two incoming calls arrived at the same time, and the telephonist connected them to the wrong callers. The adjutant handed Hitler the receiver, believing that Speer was on the line. When Hitler announced himself, 'The Führer speaking', there was a bellow of laughter from the other end. This was the paymaster who, still laughing, shouted into the receiver: 'You're crazy!' I feared an outburst of rage with serious consequences, but Hitler merely returned the receiver with the observation: 'Just someone else who thinks I'm mad.' No outward annoyance and no negative consequences followed, which I found surprising since this episode occurred after the 20 July 1944 bomb plot.

Ten days before our removal to Kniebis (FHQ Tannenberg) there was an episode at the previous FHQ at Brûly-de-Pesche, which confirmed Hitler's suspicions of the army commanders. The former Kaiser living in exile at Doorn, Holland, had sent Hitler a telegram with his congratulations to him and the German Wehrmacht 'for the enormous victory sent by God', the former Kaiser still being profoundly impressed by the French surrender. While Hitler scarcely paid the telegram any attention, some of the generals seemed to show it exaggerated respect, which Hitler naturally noticed and later, when we were alone in the bunker, imitated. Three months earlier it was not by accident that he had shied away from promoting Prince Oskar von Hohenzollern, who led a regiment at the Westwall, to the rank of general, as the Army Personnel Office had recommended.

It was quite common for him to speak disparagingly about 'the princes' and refer to them as idlers, whose only interest was their royal house. Moreover, he thought them to be the best leakers of information to abroad through their international relationships.[3] It would not surprise him in the least if one day a 'romantic' came to him with a petition to invite 'His Majesty the Kaiser' to Germany and request him 'to remain here in residence'. That this idea was

---

3 By his edict of 19 May 1943 Hitler forbade persons with international contacts (particularly members of the former ruling princely houses in Germany) from holding offices of state, in the Wehrmacht or Party, and most of these serving in the Wehrmacht were released.

by no means as unlikely as it might seem was obvious on numerous occasions. Hitler's Wehrmacht adjutant Rudolf Schmundt, head of the Army Personnel Office, attempted several times to get the Führer to promote Prince Oskar, while even Göring appeared not totally averse to such a proposition, as Hitler repeatedly had cause to remark.

The abdicated Kaiser, who spoke in his telegram of 'a change by God's hand' had surely, as Hitler pointed out sarcastically, spoken from the heart to not a few of the 'gentlemen army commanders' who would gladly have seen the inscription 'With God for Kaiser and Fatherland' on the men's belt buckles. To the question what we thought of that – we upon whose belt buckles was inscribed *Unsere Ehre Heisst Treue* – I could only reply: 'Our honour is loyalty, mein Führer'. At this, Hitler launched into a murmured monologue, something about 'tradition' and 'education', but did not deliver a full statement because the telephone interrupted him. When he answered it with his customary 'The Führer speaking', I left the room after seeing that he did not need me.

To Hitler's satisfaction the Hohenzollerns gradually distanced themselves from him soon after 1933. Prince August Wilhelm of Prussia appeared in the Berlin Garrison Church on 21 March 1933, 'Potsdam Day', with the express approval of the former kaiser in the uniform of an SA-Standartenführer, and on Göring's birthday was still wearing it even though, as he said later, he had seen how he had been deceived after the Röhm putsch of June 1934. All the same, he was the first Hohenzollern prince to declare for the NSDAP and continued as a representative and speaker for National Socialism. Obviously Hitler was interested in the content of his speeches. As an NSDAP Reichstag Deputy, he had attempted unsuccessfully through Göring to be installed as *oberpräsident* in Hanover, Brandenburg, East Prussia and Hesse.

When Prince August spoke in Nuremberg two days after Reichskristallnacht, Hitler asked for a report on what 'Prince Auwi' had said in connection with the steps arranged by Goebbels and Heydrich. These Hitler had described on 9 November 1938 as a 'spontaneous demonstration of the people's anger' which he had 'not been able to forbid'. Having just arrived from Vienna and before beginning his speech, Prince August, who must have been aware of the anti-Jewish excesses at least to some degree, had had a conversation with SA-Gruppenführer von Obernitz and had attempted to talk his way out of a ban on mentioning the event. Although von Obernitz had urged him to be wary of the 'vengeance of Goebbels and Julius Streicher', he did mention the events of the previous night in a couple of brief sentences. Remarking that he did not want to mention the events because the particulars and underlying causes were not yet available, he could nevertheless 'say with some certainty that the unlawful measures against the Jews would damage the reputation of the Reich abroad'. Hitler did not approve of this, of course, but it confirmed what he always said about the attitude of the nobility, 'abroad' in this sense being a direct pointer to the 'international links by blood'.

'And here it is again', Hitler exclaimed in the spring of 1939 after Viktor Lutze, SA chief of staff, delivered a report on what Prince August was suggesting. In January or February 1939, the prince had visited the Belgian king, Leopold III, promising that he would attempt to dissuade Hitler from war and go for a European trade deal instead. This idea was quite alien to Hitler's foreign policy aims and an interference in his realm of jurisdiction, something that only members of former ruling houses would ever dare to try. The true depth of Prince August's outrage at Kristallnacht in 1938 I was unable to determine. Whatever the case, he appeared with Hitler about a year later at a Christmas party thrown at the house of Viktoria von Dirksen, 'the mother of the Movement', whose secret hope was to see a Hohenzollern as head of state of a Hitler Reich. Whether or not Hitler avoided him I am unable to say. Even on 9 November 1942, when not only the prophets suspected where the

Third Reich was headed, Prince August still stood in Hitler's vicinity but the Führer made it clear he was not welcome there.

Hitler became estranged from the 'entire Hohenzollern clan' after an incident involving crown princess Cecilie. Immediately after concluding his first visit to Schloss Cecilienhof at Potsdam, and before he and his entourage were out of earshot, the princess had lost her self-control and commanded: 'Open the windows, it stinks in here.'[4] Nevertheless, as Julius Schaub told me later, during the second visit before taking power he had told the crown prince he would work to abolish the German federal provinces and restore the Kaiserreich with a Hohenzollern at its head, a promise apparently so transparent that the crown prince found it 'impossible to believe'. Soon after I entered service with Hitler, he invited the crown prince to visit him. On this occasion, and this showed the reversed roles, the crown prince heard a different story. Hitler told him unequivocally that there could be no question of a restoration of the Hohenzollern monarchy.[5]

King Leopold III of Belgium, who had ordered the capitulation of his country on 28 May 1940 and had voluntarily entered captivity to spare his people further bloodshed, was Hitler's guest on Obersalzberg on 19 November 1940.[6] His composure impressed Hitler, who assured him that in contrast to King Haakon VII of Norway and Queen Wilhelmina of The Netherlands, who had fled to London, his throne would be returned. He placed at King Leopold's disposal a colonel, Oberst Kiewitz, as his personal adjutant and Schloss Laaken near Brussels as his residence, where the king enjoyed great liberty

4 This Linge version was confirmed by the crown prince on 17 June 1946 while under cross-examination as a witness at Nuremberg. See Robert M.W. Kempner, *Das Dritte Reich im Kreuzverhör*, Munich and Esslingen 1969, p.113.

5 Robert M.W. Kempner, *Das Dritte Reich im Kreuzverhör*, Munich and Esslingen 1969, p.113.

6 For the record of this conversation, see Andreas Hillgruber, *Staatsmänner und Diplomaten bei Hitler*, Frankfurt/Main 1967, pp.336ff. For the conversation between Hitler and Marie-José of 17 October 1940, see ibid. pp.253ff.

under house arrest. Later Hitler changed his mind about Leopold and spoke openly of what had brought this about.

Some time after the king was received on Obersalzberg, which Marie-José, the Italian crown princess and King Leopold's sister, had arranged on 17 October 1940, Hitler remarked bitterly: 'Now I see that even this monarch is only following the politics of his royal house. His people are irrelevant.' When Kiewitz was a guest of Hitler's the following happened: I had arranged the order at table for the midday meal and placed Kiewitz near Hitler to comply with his fixed instructions that he always wanted new guests close to him. When as a matter of routine I placed the seating plan before Hitler before the meal, he surprised me by saying he wanted Reich press chief Dr Dietrich next to him and Kiewitz somewhere else. This colonel, he said, had unfortunately done what Germans tended to do too often. They forgot they were Germans quick as a flash and got into waters that they should have avoided. Kiewitz had literally turned into a monarchist and was now representing Leopold's interests as though he had become a Belgian.

As everywhere after the campaign in the West, the successes suddenly had many instigators, and it seems to me that the list has grown longer with succeeding years. In fact the true instigators of the successes, to which all those there at the time will bear witness, were Hitler and von Manstein. Independently of each other they had arrived at the same conclusion in principle and details. Just to sketch here the big picture: by a rapid occupation of Holland, they would deny Dutch sovereign territory to Britain and by an attack through Belgium and Luxemburg if possible destroy major parts of the French and British armies. Both Hitler and von Manstein rejected the OKH operational plan as next to useless and agreed on an alternative. Hitler's self-confidence helped secure these successes, but he embittered the military commanders by letting them know more clearly than before that he, 'the untrained general staff man', as he occasionally described himself, knew their trade at least as well as they did. From then on he increased his interference in their affairs until eventually it was too much.

It is unthinkable that Hitler would have treated the leading generals in 1939 or 1940 as he did in the last two years of the war. Certainly his sympathies had not been with them from the beginning, but the treatment he meted out to them from 1943 onwards would not have been accepted in 1939. He left von Manstein, co-author with himself of the quick victory in the West, in no doubt that he did not like him, although he did not dispute his military capabilities even before the campaign in the West. Hitler considered him a brilliant man technically who on the operational side 'would not allow himself to be waylaid by tradition and obsolete doctrines in his decision-making'.

Harsh judgements about military commanders could result in names being bandied about, names that Hitler did not want to hear. One of these names was Count von Schlieffen. Hitler always became incensed during the planning of the campaign in the West when the generals mentioned the name Schlieffen, whose disastrous plan was known to every student at the war academy, and during the Russian campaign he ordered that the name Schlieffen was never to be mentioned again in his presence. Moreover he ordered Scherf, the war chronicler at FHQ, never to include the name Schlieffen in any written material in the future. A number of military men such as Halder, chief of the general staff, were forced to listen as he reminded them that they had sat out the First World War on their turning stools and had never been to the front. After a situation conference at the beginning of 1940, in a rage Hitler threw down a pencil on his table and said bitterly:

> Schlieffen? These trainees in general's uniform have about as much knowledge of the practice as their beloved Schlieffen, who was never required to prove his skill as commander in the field in warfare.

Apparently you are unable to understand that the French also know him and have been taught his way of thinking.

In Russia, Hitler could not suppress his anger over such problems and could not wait until he was in private to explode: even before relative strangers he would speak out openly of his grievances and denounce the guilty parties. Thus in the autumn of 1944 he told physician Dr Erwin Giesing, who was treating him temporarily and had no affiliation to the military or the personal staff, that the defeat at Stalingrad, for which he himself shouldered the responsibility, was laid at Göring's feet. He, Göring, had assured him in December 1942 that the Luftwaffe could keep 6. Army reliably supplied for six to eight weeks, which was not the case. With troops and weapons which existed only on paper even the best commander in the field, which was what Hitler considered himself to be having regard to how things were, could not win a war. A few days before he told Giesing how he had always relied on Göring during the expansion phase of the Luftwaffe and always relied on Göring's judgement against all other advisers. He said to Giesing in my presence that the defeat of the Luftwaffe was made possible by Udet.

That man managed to produce the greatest piffle in the history of the Luftwaffe when he began designing, building and even flying aircraft himself as the general of Aircraft Supply. By doing that he so paralysed the German aviation industry for two years that during this period it came up with no new experimental designs and produced no new types.*

Udet had been obsessed by the idea of rebuilding German aviation by nationalising it. He wanted to have all aviation and

---

* For example, immediately before the outbreak of war in 1939, Heinkel flew the first pure rocket aircraft and jet-engined aircraft in demonstrations for Udet at Rostock. These revolutionary designs were not proceeded with until Messerschmitt brought out the Me 163 rocket fighter and Me 262 jet long after Udet's suicide. (TN)

the Luftwaffe in his own hands from drawing board to flight testing to mass-production, and bring it all beneath the umbrella of his Luftwaffe production office. Udet was an aficionado of the horizontal bomber and the slower but heavily armed fighter. Mölders, Galland and von Below drew my attention on a number of occasions to this error, but I would not listen to these young whelps. Göring's opinion was decisive for me.[7]

7 Quoted from Giesing's statement from 11 November 1945; document in the archive of Werner Maser.

Chapter 15

The Assassination Attempt of 1944 and Its Aftermath

T HE WAR AGAINST THE Soviet Union, which appeared necessary to Hitler from early on,[1] was led by a man of different personality to the Hitler of the previous campaigns. Certainly, long before the Polish campaign he had planned offensives against Britain and France, using Czechoslovakia and Poland as possible catalysts for these wars, but they were not so clearly impregnated with his personality, which developed through his unparalleled successes. His fundamental belief that the Reich needed the adjacent territories in the east as space essential for its existence, as a result of which a war to conquer it all was unavoidable, was encouraged by the 'wars with flowers' and the 'lightning campaigns'. The Polish campaign lasted four weeks, the French campaign six weeks. Norway and Denmark were overrun within two months, Holland in five days, Belgium seventeen days. The campaign against Yugoslavia lasted eleven days; that against Greece three weeks, although here he was forced to shore up Mussolini. This was the basis for what was to happen in the east from 22 June 1941 onwards. Without the many, and for the most part unexpected previous successes, Hitler would have been a very different man in the summer of 1941, and the war against Russia would have had another ending.

---

1 See Adolf Hitler, *Mein Kampf*, and Werner Maser, *Adolf Hitler – Legende – Mythos – Wirklichkeit*, Munich 1971, pp.231ff.

Hitler himself acted as though things were just as they had been before, but if one observed him and events closely one saw that it was not the case. The war against the Soviets, which he had declared to be an ideological war of annihilation from the outset, he pursued with fanatical ruthlessness, something that had not been seen in him from 1934 to 1941. Thus the campaign in Russia differed fundamentally from all the other wars and campaigns that he instigated. Whenever he spoke about operational plans and measures anywhere, even without hearing his voice one could make a reasonable guess as to what theatre of war he was talking about.

Despite all the versions about him to the contrary, Hitler was for me an often indulgent, reasonable and adaptable Führer, and thus it came as a brutal shock to see how he rejected Alfred Rosenberg's proposals for the treatment of the people of the Ukraine. Rosenberg, who had either not understood Hitler's intentions and objectives, or wanted to deflect them elsewhere, had made a great effort to win Hitler over for his personal policies in the Ukraine. In vain. The Führer preferred the 'policies' of Erich Koch, who wanted to rule with the whip – and did so. Usually cinema newsreels had their effect on Hitler, and he would often make a decision subsequent to seeing one. I was present when he saw the film of our troops marching into the Ukraine. They were received as liberators with flowers, bread and salt. Hitler's face was impassive. His features were relaxed. Just for a second they might register a small surprise. Suddenly as I was observing him his face hardened. I looked at the screen and saw the reason: Ukrainian women, children and the old were crossing themselves, crucifix in hand. In Poland, France, Belgium and Holland he would have frowned at such pictures, but here it was quite different.

We all knew that the primary military resistance to Hitler, which had not been the only subject of discussions in the spring of 1938, had fermented further. It was also obvious to us that this resistance would be fuelled by every operational failure, every battlefield defeat and every victim in the homeland. That it would lead to an assassination attempt with a large-scale conspiracy was something none of us feared for it had been too much talked of around Hitler. Too often Himmler's confidante Fegelein had warned of it self-importantly and demanded 'special security measures'.

When the Allied invasion began in June 1944 Fegelein took me aside and told me 'under a pledge of secrecy' that they were 'on the trail' of a conspiracy. It involved, so he said, mainly 'disaffected officers above all from the nobility'. Himmler, his chief, was playing along with one of these groups so as to strike at the right moment. Fegelein said that I should be especially watchful and not let the Führer out of my sight. As I knew Fegelein's bloated idea of himself I did not take the thing seriously, especially since it was my duty to watch over Hitler carefully anyway.

During Hitler's visit to Zeitzler, chief of the army general staff, the SS bodyguard, officers of the general staff and I sat together in conversation. Some of the Wehrmacht officers present expressed their belief quite openly that they doubted the war could still be won, especially since Hitler was not running it as they would have liked. The SS officers did not share their pessimism and advised their Wehrmacht comrades to be more discreet in future. I could not share their negative outlook, for I was convinced that Hitler still had the necessary authority to overcome interior resistance. Letters from discharged officers reinforced me in this opinion. I read how von Brauchitsch had written after his dismissal that despite all difficulties Hitler's genius would lead the German Wehrmacht to victory. That the Foreign Ministry was already conducting 'peace negotiations' in Stockholm I discovered only after the attempt of 20 July 1944.

On our return to FHQ Wolfsschanze we found a changed picture. The conversion work was almost complete. It looked like Ancient Egypt, the massive bunkers had a pyramid look about them. The Führer-bunker was not yet ready, and Hitler had to move into the so-called guest's bunker which had reinforced accommodation.

The situation conferences were to be held in a barrack hut with protection only against shrapnel.

On 20 July 1944 – a fine summer's day – Hitler was expecting a visit from Mussolini. For this reason the military conference had been advanced to 1230 hours. At that time I was about 100 metres away, discussing details of the forthcoming Mussolini visit with the head of protocol, von Dörnberg and other officials. Suddenly there was an explosion. We continued our talk, assuming that Hitler's German Shepherd, which had the run of the place, had set off one of the landmines which surrounded FHQ for its security. It was exactly 1250 hours. A few minutes later an orderly came running to our room and cried in a trembling voice: 'Hauptsturmführer Linge, go at once to the Führer!' I sensed immediately that something terrible had occurred. As I was running to Hitler's bunker, Major von Freyend, Keitel's adjutant, came up at the trot. He was greatly distressed, blood running down his face. Horrified I asked what had happened. He gasped: 'The Führer is alive and is in the small dining room of the bunker.' When I got there Hitler looked at me questioningly with great eyes and noticed my concerned expression. With a calm smile he said: 'Linge, somebody tried to kill me'.

His uniform was in ribbons. His hair was singed and hung down in strands. My knees were trembling, but he acted as though nothing had happened. He was sitting on the round table. From his bared legs Dr Hasselbach removed 200 wood splinters and dressed his wounds. Hitler's right arm hung down limply. His face and legs were still bleeding, but nothing else suggested the violence of the event. Hasselbach told me later that Hitler's pulse had been quite normal. This was something he could not understand. Hitler was preoccupied feverishly asking himself who had planted the bomb and where it had been made. He had noticed, he said, that as it exploded the tongue of flame had a different colour to German explosives. One must consider that this bomb was of British origin.

He also claimed that immediately after the explosion he had looked at the people present in the hut and those arriving immediately after the explosion to see if any betrayed by their facial expressions their complicity in the event. While under treatment by Dr Hasselbach he told me: 'I have to consider that explosives may have been concealed in my bunker, and I would ask you to have the floors and walls searched immediately.' After I had passed this order to the RSD,[2] for the first time in my long service with him I helped him change his clothing. Then I went to the barrack hut to see the 'crime scene' for myself. There were still some soldiers outside, groaning. Berger, the stenographer who had been seated opposite Hitler, was dead. The bomb had torn off his legs. The chief of the Luftwaffe general staff, whose legs had been crushed, was groaning close to death. He and Dr Karl Brandt, who had been standing next to Hitler and had taken most of the blast, died immediately afterwards. Schmundt, who lost an eye and a leg, died two weeks later in the military hospital at Rastenburg.

Soon afterwards it was clear to Hitler who had brought the bomb into the hut: Stauffenberg. The events had played out like this: shortly before the explosion, General Buhle had asked me in some excitement if a telephone call for him arranged by Stauffenberg had been put through yet. I said no, at which Buhle had become extremely annoyed. Hitler heard about this, and unlike the RSD drew the correct inference at once and asked his Luftwaffe adjutant von Below 'where this Oberst Stauffenberg came from'. When he was told, 'The count is one of Generaloberst Fromm's men', he responded enraged: 'Then Stauffenberg is the assassin'. Suspicions had fallen at first – not from Hitler – on the bunker workers. Peter

---

2 The RSD (Reichssicherheitsdienst) was a unit formed in March or April 1933 of eight Munich detectives as a protection squad for the Reich Chancellery and later the FHQs. Its chief was a lieutenant from the Bavarian provincial police, Johann Rattenhuber who remained in post throughout. By 1944 the force was 250 strong, thirty being support staff. Its deputy commander was SS Obersturmbannführer Peter Högl.

Högl, RSD chief at FHQ, had had them all arrested, but after Hitler's remark about Stauffenberg they were released. Nobody was allowed to leave FHQ, however; Högl had closed all the exits.

Whether Stauffenberg was still inside the FHQ complex we had no idea. He had awaited the explosion away from the hut and proceeded to the main gate where a sentry had stopped him. Precisely informed of FHQ procedures and wanting to fly back to Berlin at once he had played the rank card and had himself put through to the camp commandant's adjutant, a Rittmeister and therefore inferior in rank. As Hitler discovered later, with great self-confidence and 'certain of victory' Stauffenberg had demanded: 'What do you need? You know that my aircraft is waiting for me. I have strict orders from the Führer personally to convey an important report from the Führer to Generaloberst Fromm as soon as possible. Do you wish to accept the consequences of any delay?' That the officer allowed him to pass was understandable under the circumstances. Not even Hitler censured his action.

It had not been possible to inform the aerodrome by telephone to stop Stauffenberg's flight. The lines were destroyed. FHQ was also cut off from Berlin. This had been ordered by General Fellgiebel, Head of OKH Signals. Meanwhile the man who had driven Stauffenberg to the aerodrome was arrested. He stated that on the way his passenger had thrown a packet out of the car. This packet was recovered and found to contain explosives.

While the first interrogations were taking place, Hitler drove to Görlitz railway station within the complex to meet Mussolini. On the way he said: 'It is good that the Duce will see me immediately after the attempt on my life.' Calm and composed, he was determined to meet Mussolini as if nothing out of the ordinary had happened. As they stood together on the platform I saw the Duce look in consternation at Hitler's right arm, which he had in a black sling. They spoke German together. Hitler explained 'in passing' that an attempt had just been made to kill him. He led Mussolini, appalled, to the scene and narrated the event to him. Horrified, speechless, Mussolini shook his head. They faced each other amongst the wreckage and Hitler said: 'When I go over it in my mind and think that everybody received serious injuries except me, that some even lost their lives, I have to say that I have escaped death in a miraculous manner. This makes me certain that nothing can happen to me, that Providence has selected me to conclude our common aim victoriously.' Visibly affected, Mussolini assured him: 'I am totally of your opinion. It is a sign from heaven.' Repeatedly he shook Hitler's hands and congratulated him on his escape.

At the meal arranged for Mussolini's visit, Göring, Himmler, Ribbentrop and others were present. Only upon their arrival at FHQ had they learned what had happened. They rather overdid the expressions of sympathy and their 'loyalty to the Führer', Göring especially being unable to restrain himself, embracing the Führer emotionally and saying: 'Thank God, mein Führer, that you have been preserved for us!' Grave and immobile Hitler replied: 'This attempt was aimed not only at me. This day was chosen to kill us all. These conspirators have nothing of the revolutionary in them. They are not even rebels! If this Stauffenberg had drawn a pistol and shot me down, then he would have been a man. But instead he is a miserable coward!'

Himmler flew at once to Berlin to take the steps necessary to put down the rebellion, arrest Stauffenberg and all those implicated in the plot. I had to connect Hitler to Goebbels. Hitler wanted to know what was going on in Berlin. Because of the destruction it took hours to get through. Hitler then informed Goebbels of the event. In great excitement he asked if Berlin was calm. Goebbels reported that Major Remer, commander of the Berlin Guard Batallion, was at his side. Goebbels had told him to occupy the government district since he, Goebbels, had no orders and did not know what he should do. Hitler promoted Remer to colonel on the spot and said that he wanted to talk to him. He said: 'Remer, there has been an attempt to kill me, but I have survived. My orders, and only my orders, are valid! Understood? You have to secure Berlin. Use all methods you consider necessary. Shoot everybody who does not obey my orders!'

After a short conversation with Goebbels he hung up and went with Mussolini to see the workers reinforcing the bunkers. He told them that he had known from the outset that the assassin could never have come from amongst them. 'My enemies', he said, 'were always the "vons" who call themselves aristocrats.' The scheduled talks with Mussolini never took place. Mussolini left: it was their last meeting.

From May 1945 onwards everybody who had spent any time with Hitler was required to oblige the victorious powers – sometimes under torture – with his or her assessment of Hitler. This included Erwin Giesing. His forced judgement of Hitler, prepared on 11 November 1945, read:

> . . . Ascetic and demagogic, a Roman-type tribune of the people and dictator, later madness of the Caesars and a tyrant. The success of the attempt of 20 July 1944 would only have had an advantage for Germany, Europe and the world if Hitler's political satellites Himmler and Bormann, Ribbentrop and Göring, Keitel and Fegelein – and all the others – had become with him . . . victims of the attempt, for in the case of his death the ensuing violent internal struggle and civil war would perhaps have plunged Germany into even greater misery than the senseless continuation of the war in the face of unavoidable military defeat has done.[3]

Bormann had his days of greatness in July 1944. Himmler and Kaltenbrunner could well be envious, and were. While they rounded up the circle of conspirators and searched for evidence, in a flash

---

3 Erwin Giesing, notes, 11 November 1945, document in archive of Werner Maser.

Bormann took over the Party apparatus. In his hands, confidence was guaranteed and Hitler could be relieved of any remaining worries. One telex after another streamed out with guidelines from Bormann and advice from Bormann, giving recipients the impression that 'up top everything is in excellent order just as before'. Hitler, dominated by the lust for revenge and a destructive urge, owed much to Bormann. Knowing that Bormann was playing his part as never before Hitler could devote some of his energies to the persecution and punishment of the conspirators.

How sceptically Hitler viewed every report is shown by the following example: I was standing beside him when he was told that Generaloberst Fromm had had Stauffenberg and Olbricht shot in Berlin. Outwardly calm, but very wound up, he listened to the report. 'Fromm had Stauffenberg executed?' he murmured. Then he ordered: 'Dig him up, dig up Stauffenberg immediately.' After the exhumation had confirmed that Stauffenberg had indeed been the victim, Hitler did not react as Bormann had expected, but concluded spontaneously: 'Fromm is the leader. This is how he got rid of his accomplices and those who could put him in the frame.' It was not only Bormann who was visibly shocked at this statement. Hitler, noticing our reactions, added simply: 'I know my Pappenheimer.'* This ended the preliminary enquiry.

Fromm, who later defended himself very skilfully before the People's Court, initially escaped with his life but Hitler's rage caught up with him on 19 March 1945 when he was executed on the Führer's personal order.

I was more than a little dejected when I saw on Hitler's table the list of names of those arrested on suspicion of belonging to

---

* This was a notorious witch hunt in Munich in the year 1600 when a murderer deflected suspicion from himself on the innocent Pappenheimer family. Under dreadful torture they confessed not only to the murderer's crime but also to all the other unsolved felonies in the province over recent years, and were executed in a most cruel and inhuman manner. (TN)

the circle of conspirators or being implicated. One of these was Oberstleutnant Smend from Zeitzler's staff. I knew him and some of the other accused. One day Hitler received a letter from Smend. He read it in my presence and was at first very pensive. Smend had shown courage. He wrote to Hitler that since Stalingrad the opinion had spread openly through the staff that the war could no longer be won with Hitler because his abilities to lead fell short of what was required. 'This man at least writes like a soldier', Hitler remarked and added, 'and he does not beg for his life.' As he went on reading, however, his features darkened. Smend blamed his superiors for not having taken younger officers such as himself in hand and shown them how to have faith in the Führer. He gave the impression that he and his ilk were officers who had been hopelessly misled, and of whom too much had been asked, who like schoolchildren had been waiting for the saving words of their teacher. This was too much for Hitler, who had trusted in and built on the spirit of the young and younger officers. Smend's fate was sealed. I am certain not only that his life would have been spared, but also that he might have been acquitted if he had not written in so pathetic a way as to blame and denounce his superior officers. My impression was that the letter rekindled Hitler's lust for vengeance, and I am as convinced now as I was then that many of the accused would have received a different sentence from Freisler if Smend's letter had been 'manly' throughout, as Hitler described it.

Hitler had kept himself informed of the proceedings in the People's Court through film, photos, bulletins and oral reports. Initially he only spat out the names Witzleben, Goerdeler, Höpfner, Fellgiebel, Haase, Hassel and von der Schulenburg, although he did make the bitter observation: 'Pity that Schulenburg, a man with so much backbone, was not on my side.' However improbable it may sound, it is nevertheless true: Hitler went to great lengths in his search for 'positive glimmers of light in this swamp' as he once said. As he saw it, all the accused merited their fate. He wanted to see them hang 'like cattle', he said, after reading reports on their conduct and statements. Thirty-five years later, on 18 May 1979, the *Frankfurter Allgemeine Zeitung* published an extract from a dialogue between Roland Freisler and Hans Bernd von Haeften. I had read it, as did Hitler, in 1944.

> **Freisler (Fr):** Do you not understand that when a nation is fighting for its very life, if one of the probably thousands of colonels in the army of that nation has such an opinion, that it is treason to depart in any way from loyalty to the Führer?
>
> **Haeften (Ha):** I no longer recognise this duty of loyalty.
>
> **Fr:** Aha! So it is clear, you do not recognise it, and so you say, if I do not have that duty of loyalty, I cannot look on it as treason.
>
> **Ha:** No, not quite. But in the light of the world-historical view of the Führer's role which I have, er . . . that is to say, he is a great proponent of evil, I was of the view . . .
>
> **Fr:** Well yes, you need say no more.
>
> **Ha:** *Jawohl.*
>
> **Fr:** A fine person to have in the Foreign Service. Then I would ask you another question: you had the gall to be an official in the Foreign Ministry?
>
> **Ha:** Yes.
>
> **Fr:** Yes.

Now and again Haeften had crossed my path. I had seen him on different occasions but did not actually know him. After I had 'studied' his 'appearance' before the People's Court, though very much hamstrung by the circumstances and the conduct of those who thought like him, of whom Hitler had wanted to rid himself, I understood Hitler's orders for 'lightning fast' decisions, judgements within two hours, and his demand that the accused were not to be allowed to make speeches. The fact that the proceedings at the time were accepted by overseas jurists and journalists as unobjectionable from the juristic point of view contributed to a great extent to the lack of protest at there being no proper trial. The accused did not deny their complicity and had to expect execution in the event that their plot failed.

Hitler's reaction when told on 20 July 1944 that in the army command in Paris, under the roof of Stülpnagel and Kluge, his death had been prematurely celebrated with champagne needs no description from me. The suicide of Rommel in October 1944 and Kluge's suicide were connected events known about for years. I mention these two names because they meant more to Hitler than is generally known.[4]

Rommel's suicide was obviously his own decision, but Hitler doubted that Kluge's suicide had been voluntary. He suspected that 'the English poisoned him' after they had 'failed to convince the Generalfeldmarschall to come over to their side'. He even asked Frau Kluge for permission to autopsy the body of her husband. The result did not bear out his suspicion. Kluge had taken his own life. This was another heavy blow for Hitler, now constantly being urged by Himmler in the background 'to exterminate the whole gang'.

That special security measures were introduced after 20 July goes without saying. Only about sixty people, whose names Hitler had listed personally, were permitted access to him without a prior body search. Briefcases and such-like had to be left behind. Although I saw the need for such measures, they depressed me. Generals, colonels, staff officers, lieutenants, NCOs and simple privates with the highest decorations came – men who had risked their lives for Hitler – and had to be patted down by the RSD like convicted thieves. Numerous 'visitors' declared that they 'considered it finally necessary' to have to go through this procedure, but I was not happy to see it every day. Soldiers with gold close-combat clasps, gold wound badges, Iron Crosses and Knights Crosses, often still in their

---

4 For Rommel see e.g. David Irving, *Rommel, Eine Biographie*, Hamburg 1978.

uniforms direct from the front, had to be frisked for weapons like gangsters. Until then I had never acted off my own bat, but now I did. I went to Högl and told him that the Führer had ordered such searches to be discontinued if the visitor was highly decorated. This was done. When Hitler heard of my unauthorised 'measure', which could naturally have had the most serious consequences for me, he said nothing but merely looked at me and made me realise my position. Feeling very uncertain, I explained: 'Mein Führer, what would a man think who arrives from the front to receive his Knights Cross and is frisked beforehand like a convicted murderer?' Hitler's reaction confirmed what I had experienced of him time and again: he would allow pre-emptive decisions if they seemed justified.

A 'glimmer of light' in the 'swamp' now appeared to him in the shape of Generalfeldmarschall Keitel, whose 'unpolitical way of thinking and lack of initiative' was something of which Hitler had been a regular critic. Overnight there was a completely different Keitel. When Hitler had to confine himself to bed as a result of the attempt on his life, it was not to Bormann or Himmler that he handed affairs but to Keitel. He who until then had been only the obedient and powerless general proved at once that he merited his high military rank and his impressive position. Prudent, decisive, unperturbed by the intercessions of Himmler and Bormann, he laid down what had to be done until Hitler was fit to take back the reins of power alone. When Hitler was on the road to recovery, he resumed his short walks in the FHQ terrain, usually accompanied by myself and constantly by Blondi, his intelligent and lively German Shepherd.

One day during one such stroll, unfortunately I do not recall the date but it was after 20 July 1944. Hitler broached the subject of peace negotiations. As I was merely a listener, he did not need answers to his questions, so as was his custom he could develop his ideas without interruption. He did not finish off, though, and for no apparent reason changed the subject. When we were in his small private room, Hewel's representative and Albert Bormann, Martin Bormann's brother, appeared. Hitler had them remain standing at the door, a comical situation, the two of them were blocking the exit. Whatever Hitler was intending was not clear to me. Apparently he wanted me present as a witness without actually saying so. Uncertainly, very cautiously, Albert Bormann and his colleague began their reports on the 'peace negotiations' in Stockholm. Hitler listened for a while in silence. When Albert Bormann stated that the Allies were not prepared to enter serious negotiations so long as he, Hitler, remained head of state, the NSDAP continued to exist and the German forces were not ready to accept unconditional surrender, Hitler bristled. Providence, he retorted angrily, had not kept him alive on 20 July from caprice. As before he had been chosen and remained in position to give positive form to Germany's future. His enemies knew what outcome their conditions would have. He was therefore no longer prepared to allow the negotiations to proceed, he ordered, and without any further ado he dismissed the pair of them.

The 20 July 1944 plot not only brought about a major change in Hitler's life. I was quickly saddled with tasks that Stauffenberg's bomb initiated. New faces appeared. One of these was the intelligent and pleasant ENT specialist Dr Erwin Giesing, called in to treat Hitler. He informed the US Secret Service on 11 November 1945:

> . . . My impression on meeting Hitler for the first time on 22 July 1944 was not of a 'powerful and feared man' with 'fascinating' or even 'hypnotic' personality. The impression he made on me was of a prematurely old, almost depleted and exhausted man trying to keep going on the vestiges of his strength. I was not impressed very much by his allegedly 'penetrating eyes' or his predicted masterful or even tyrannical personality which I had expected from the press, radio, personal accounts and the reports of others.[5]

5 Quoted from Giesing's statement of 11 November 1945, document in archive of Werner Maser.

Giesing, who treated Hitler in fifty to sixty sessions between 22 July and 7 October 1944 reacted much as I had on my first meeting with Hitler. He saw nothing unusual in the Führer's vaunted eyes. Yet he succumbed to Hitler totally. We had many conversations in which we searched for the 'reasons' but never found them.

Giesing was a man whom Hitler accepted not only as a physician. He spoke with him about God and the world and would even allow Giesing to contradict him. Of this Giesing said later:

> Because Hitler allowed me to contradict him quite often is no proof that he would allow others to do so. Additionally he was a much too powerful political figure and too firmly convinced of the absolute rightness of his opinions, and he would never have tolerated anybody almost equally clever or gifted near him. He had this simple belief that he understood most things better, and could do most things better, than other people. I watched how he controlled himself and concentrated during our conversations when . . . differences of opinion occurred. Whoever . . . had the misfortune to bring bad news fell . . . into a certain discredit disadvantageous for his position and future. For that reason facts were often 'tarted up' and events given a better slant. Hitler was convinced almost exclusively by statistics and he loved to have things advocated to him in percentages or by other figurework. From this there arose a way of falsely accounting for all manner of things which he could never verify himself or had not requested.[6]

Giesing, unlike myself, had never had to be the bearer of bad news. On the contrary, his treatment quickly alleviated Hitler's suffering and injuries. He – the 'bringer of good news' – could if necessary initiate conversations in which there were no negative aspects, which Hitler would not be keen to know. Hitler himself

6 Ibid.

would only give his attention to negative themes once they could no longer be ignored. Thus the doctor saw himself as an observer who finally gave advice if it needed to be taken into account. For me, Giesing was a gain. He did not belong in the intimate circle, had no contact with it, and therefore they did not attempt to befriend him. He drew my attention to matters relating to Hitler and his way of life to which until then I had hardly attached any importance, or none at all. What had been the custom for years, and was therefore not questioned, often struck Giesing as interesting medically. Thus he wrote:

> On my first examinations I noticed . . . that in Hitler's room Linge only ever turned on one bulb in the lamp standard. He . . . said that Hitler could not stand bright light and for about eighteen months he had always had only one bulb burning in the room. For the purpose of my medical investigation the low lighting was very welcome since with such poor illumination I could arrange the best lighting for the examination. After my own examination lamp was turned off, and the standard lamp turned on, I noticed very clearly how poor the lighting was in the room.

In this gloom Hitler read and worked, even though he had needed spectacles to read small print since 1936. Giesing tried to change the way Hitler did things but was unsuccessful, and Giesing, who liked steak and cutlets, also failed to convince Hitler that his large energy consumption made it necessary for him to start including egg white, meat and animal fats again in his diet.

Giesing made every effort to exercise positive influences on Hitler but was as little successful as all 'advisers' before and after him. After one examination he came to me complaining about the discrepancy between Hitler's knowledge and his application of this knowledge. 'The Führer talks to me like a medical specialist about problems of nutrition and other questions but never considers that he should put his knowledge into practice with himself.'

That was Hitler's way. He would hold back stubbornly from doing something he had decided upon, even when he felt the disadvantages in his own body. In the same way that nobody could convince him to wear a different service cap, so it was impossible to convince him that it was in his own interests to change his diet, to keep regular hours and sleep normally, to take exercise and live a more healthy life in other respects. When Giesing once suggested, after diagnosing one of Hitler's headaches as being due to inflammation, that he needed a change of climate and should leave East Prussia in favour of at least a temporary stay at Berchtesgaden, he gave 'important political grounds' as the reason for declining. 'Clinically and medically', he told Giesing, 'your opinion is well founded, but for political considerations I cannot leave my HQ in East Prussia.' Then he explained to him the reason that, if he should leave the province, the East Prussians would 'justly' accuse him of abandoning them to the Russians. However secretly he might undertake a change of location, 'somehow as always' it would become known. To cause anxiety in East Prussia was the last thing he would wish. Therefore he had to remain at Wolfsschanze. Besides, in the event of a removal to Berchtesgaden the people would think he was going back to his private apartment, leaving the conduct of the war to the generals and the government of the country to the ministers.

In fact he did more to tire himself out on the Berg than anywhere else. Looking at me he asked: 'Linge, you have seen me for ten years now. Haven't I always been a glutton for work?' I had to agree, for I had never seen him loafing. Lazybones Hitler, who killed time travelling, chatting, listening to records, watching films and sleeping, is a character of fantasy in some of the biographies of him. He was in reality a workhorse with limitless energy, a person who even at table had only work in his head. His guests listened to him attentively, and not a few of them were convinced that through him they had been 'afforded a look into Paradise through a side door'. During the war he tried desperately to dissociate himself from work in conversations which were actually monologues. That he failed in this I discovered often, for while he would hold forth on some question 'nothing to do with the war' he would be thinking all the while how he could bring this or that operational change into play at the front. He could hardly expect his guests, even though they had a very great interest in the war, to listen to him talking about ships' armour, aircraft equipment, obsolete weapons and units, he said. Every soldier who had been at the front knew what soldiers liked to talk about best in their free time.

Giesing's urgent medical advice to Hitler that he should spend at least four to six weeks immediately at Obersalzberg was brushed aside as 'out of the question'. When Giesing, not a man to give up lightly, pressed the matter later, Hitler told him that the transport of the entire FHQ and OKH apparatus, which would be the enforced consequence of a 'change of climate', was unreasonable for such a brief period, and anyway there was no chance of 'continuity' nor a 'peaceful work atmosphere' there. With the observation, 'So you see, doctor, I have to stay here,' the subject of 'a change of climate', of which I was understandably very much in favour from a personal point of view, came to nothing.

There was a dramatic event on the afternoon of 1 October 1944 during an examination of Hitler by Dr Giesing. He wrote about it himself on 12 June 1946:

Hitler pushed back the bed covers and drew up his night shirt so that I could examine his body. He was generally somewhat emaciated and I detected a distinct meteorism (build up of intestinal gases). There was no sensitivity to touch in the stomach region. The right side of the upper abdomen and gall bladder regions were not painful when depressed. The peritoneal reflexes when tested with a needle seemed very responsive. I then requested Hitler to submit to a neurological control examination to which he agreed. I covered the abdomen with a night shirt and pulled away the bed clothing. I found no abnormalities of the genitals. Babinski, Gordon, Rossolimeau and Oppenheim reflexes negative. I did not carry out a Rombergs test . . . but I would have expected this to have been negative bearing in mind the other results. I asked Hitler to take off his nightshirt, which he did with the help of Linge and myself. The pallid skin was fairly dry with no sweat in the armpits. The triceps and arm reflexes were very responsive either side, the spastic reflexes of the upper extremities negative. There was no adiadochokinesis or other cerebral symptoms: on examination of the facialis reflex by tapping before the salival gland I observed a Chvostek reflex: Kernig and Lasegne definitely negative, no trace of stiffness of the neck, free movement of the head in all directions. The musculature of the upper arm seemed to me to have a certain rigidity in quick movements, bending and stretching . . . Hitler followed this neurological examination with great interest and then said to me: 'Apart from nervous excitability I have a quite sound nervous system, and I hope that everything will be well again quite soon. Even the intestinal cramps are easing off. Yesterday and the day before Morell gave me a camomile enema to obtain stools and later he will do another . . . I have been able to eat next to nothing over the last three days so that the intestine is practically empty . . . and has had a good rest.' Linge and I helped Hitler re-dress. Then he said: 'Now for entertainment we must not forget the treatment. Please have a look in my nose and put in the cocaine stuff. My throat is a little better but I am still hoarse.' I usually gave the ten per cent cocaine solution in the left nostril. Next I examined his ears and throat. After a few minutes Hitler said: 'Now my head is clear and I feel so well that I could get up soon except that I am very thin which is the result of the intestinal cramps and not eating.' A few moments later I noticed that he had closed his eyes and lost the facial flush he had had. I took his pulse, which was rapid and weak, about 90, the quality seemed to me significantly weaker than previously. I asked Hitler how he felt, but he made no reply. It was clear he had suffered a slight collapse in which one could not get through to him. Linge had gone to the door to answer a sharp knock . . . it must have been only a few moments that I was alone with Hitler, for when Linge came back I was still administering the cocaine in the left nostril . . . Linge stood at the foot of the bed and asked how much longer I would be. I said: 'I have finished'. At this moment Hitler's face became paler, and there were some spasmodic facial contortions. He also drew up his legs. When Linge saw this, he said: 'The Führer's intestinal convulsions are returning, leave him in peace now. He will probably sleep.' We collected up the instruments and quickly left his bedroom.[7]

Actually Hitler looked gravely ill. He was very weak and fell asleep quickly. Giesing waited awhile, advised me what to do in the event of a recurrence and made me swear to tell nobody what had transpired. Then he left Hitler, whom I now had to keep isolated more than ever before. I did not dare inform Bormann or Himmler. If Hitler were needed, I had to call Giesing first. Fortunately that was unnecessary. Hitler was soon back on his feet. This incident bound me to Giesing as if we were conspirators. I learned from him what he considered Hitler's condition to be, about which Hitler had spoken to him in previous weeks and what he had told him behind closed doors. I had not been present at any of these examinations and conversations. My observations and Giesing's medical commentary on the situation confirmed that Hitler had never been so ill and near death as he had been in October 1944, external circumstances apart.

After this circulatory collapse Hitler had gone downhill rapidly, and when we were alone he admitted it. I had to describe to him how it seemed to me when he 'suddenly fell away'. He replied: 'Yes,

---

7 Werner Maser, *Adolf Hitler – Legende – Mythos – Wirklichkeit*, Munich 1971, pp.390ff

just a fraction of a second and one is through. One does not need to fear it.' That I was never to speak to anybody about his condition he considered so obvious that he did not even bother to caution me. I can only wonder what might have happened if for example Himmler had known how ill Hitler had been. The Führer relieved doctors Brandt and Hasselbach of their positions and Giesing also appeared for the last time on 7 October 1944. Only Morell was retained, joined on 31 October by SS physician Dr Ludwig Stumpfegger on Himmler's recommendation. Hitler would accept medication only from my hand. His distrust was getting excessive. From the beginning of October he could hear the content of whispered conversations at five to six steps distance, but that did nothing to alleviate his suspicions, which made everyone's life hell. If I had not had strong nerves it might have been difficult to cope with it.

A ray of light burst on the scene on 16 December 1944 when our troops embarked on the Ardennes Offensive, masterfully prepared and kept wonderfully secret. It started off very well, and Hitler seemed to revive. He had gained strength a little, was speaking normally again, was more confident and looked more vigorous. His face had a greyish pallor, however, and when he walked he stooped, and shuffled slightly. The whole left side of his body trembled. If he looked into the light his eyes hurt. All this would only be noticed by somebody who had spent a lot of time in his presence. In short meetings he was able to hide the weakness and his pain, and he did so. It had only been five weeks since we had left East Prussia, that wonderful province with its cultivated expanses, its picturesque lakes and dark woods, but to me it seemed to be years.

Chapter 16

1945 – The Last Months of the Third Reich: Reflections on Russia

AFTER OUR DECEMBER 1944 victories on the Western Front led to nothing, a mood overtook everybody in which all hope of a possible change in the war situation were dashed. Lethargy spread like a sea mist and depressed us all, even Hitler, who showed it only when I was alone with him. Even when Bormann put in an appearance, he would change his facial expression and pretend that 'everything is in order'. Morell he could not fool. He saw the deterioration in his patient. In mid-February 1945 Giesing returned to the HQ. I was very happy to see him again since I knew he always had a positive effect on Hitler. Now I hoped he could uplift him again. I requested Hitler to receive him. Annoyed since the beginning of October 1944 at Giesing's 'infringements of jurisdiction', as he called them, Hitler was undecided and said neither yes nor no which meant to me 'arrange a chance meeting'. I did this. During an air raid alarm I arranged for Giesing to more or less collide with Hitler. With the doctor standing in his path, Hitler looked up and said pleasantly, 'Ah, doctor, how are you and your family? Come with me!' The old low mood was swept away. Hitler looked pleased, unforced, natural. He knew that he could not conceal from Giesing the rapid onset of the process of deterioration which had occurred during Giesing's absence.

Giesing's report speaks for itself:

Now that I saw Hitler's face [he wrote in 1945] I was amazed at the change. He seemed to have aged and was more stooped than ever. His facial complexion was pallid and he had large bags under his eyes. His speech was clear but soft. I noticed at once a pronounced trembling of the left arm and hand which was worse if the hand was not supported, so that Hitler always rested the arm on the table or his hands on the chair seat . . . I had the impression that he was fairly far away mentally and not so concentrated as formerly. I had the impression of a man absolutely exhausted and absent. His hands were very pale and his fingernails bloodless.[1]

Hitler left Berlin on his last drive to the front at the beginning of March 1945. Our car drove over ploughed fields, pasture and meadow to Stettin, which was still held by German forces. It needed all his physical energy to endure, but he would not give in. Crossing ploughed land one morning to reach a Luftwaffe command post, suddenly the farmers were around us with their wives. They seemed to have forgotten the close thunder of the Russian artillery. They had apparently not expected to see him, Hitler, right at the front, and one felt at once the effect that Hitler had on them even though he was now old, greying, bent and degenerating. He did not speak to them, but gave a jovial wave. For a moment I saw us back in the epoch of our picnic excursions. The same faces as then, the hopes we once had: 'The Führer will find a way'. There was nothing else to explain the behaviour of the people here. That Hitler created strength for himself from these encounters was sensed not only by me but also noticed by General Burgdorf, Schaub and Bormann, who regularly accompanied Hitler.

During the Russian campaign in the winter of 1941, Hitler went to Feldmarschall von Reichenau's army group. I knew from private

---

1 Werner Maser, *Adolf Hitler – Legende – Mythos – Wirklichkeit*, Munich 1971, p.394.

meetings between them at the Berg that Reichenau understood something about painting, which pleased Hitler immensely. Harmoniously and knowledgably they discussed the oil paintings hung at the Berghof. Politically Reichenau was close to Hitler, and occasionally he visited Hitler in civilian clothing, a sure sign of a certain favouritism. After our flight to the front, soldiers were waiting in a large hall to greet Hitler, visibly pleased to see him in person. At the meal table a simple soldier sat at his left, at his right an NCO. He conversed freely with everybody. Afterwards he gave a speech in which he recalled that the German kaisers of the Middle Ages had always been drawn to the south, to Italy. This time, under his leadership, German troops would conquer a country whose soil offered everything Germany needed.

With applause resounding around the hall we headed for our quarters, the ground floor of a house. His room had a large window which nobody could avoid passing when entering or leaving the building. Before I worked out the reason of this odd constructional design, Hitler explained that a political informer, installed as a house guard, had lived there. His job had been to watch the occupants of the house. I was always unable to conceal my private thoughts and must have pulled an incredulous face, for Hitler took me by the arm, pushed me out of the room and drew my attention to the skylights above all the doors. I now observed that every room had its own skylight through which the building snooper could ascertain what the people inside 'were up to'.

We did not know when we would be returning to FHQ, and Hitler was therefore very unsettled. He was waiting nervously for reports from other army groups which could not reach him through von Reichenau, because there was no telephone link between the respective army groups. He had no alternative but to return to FHQ where all reports and information were collated. It was clear to me then that in future he could leave FHQ very seldom if he wanted to lead successfully, but nevertheless he undertook further trips to the front to Uman and Kiev in his search for immediate contact with the fighting troops. Whenever he met foot soldiers on such trips he would usually stop the car and ask the infantry where they came from, their units and how they felt as his soldiers. He would generally ask how they liked 'the Workers' and Peasants' Paradise' and whether he, their supreme Führer, had misled them about it. No matter from where they originated, to this latter question they would always answer, 'No, it is much worse!' For the midday meal with the soldiers, tables and benches would be set up. Hitler would have a plate of pea soup, the meat having been removed beforehand. He and I would go directly to the field kitchen and ladle out our pea soup together.

One of the excursions to the front took us to Smolensk, another to Zaporozhe, where there was a dramatic incident. While Hitler was in conference with his generals, the airfield where our aircraft were parked came under Russian attack, with the result that part of it was captured. The report came as a shock for us and in confusion, lacking any experience of the front, we waited anxiously to see how Hitler would handle the situation. We had the report passed to him at once. It amazed us to see that he could hardly be bothered with it, this report which had hurled us all into a state of near panic. Issuing a few pithy instructions as to how the problem was to be cleared up, he quietly resumed his conference. If the Russians had got wind of Hitler's presence this affair would probably have turned out rather differently.

The longest front flight was in 1943, to Rostov on the Black Sea. Hitler flew the first leg in his well-known Fw 200 Condor, then in the actual front area he boarded a Messerschmitt production aircraft in which only he, General Schmundt, Dr Morell and I could be squeezed. German fighters escorted us at an altitude of 3,000–4,000 metres. Hitler was calm and had no fear. Now and again he glanced at the fighter escort knowing that he could rely on them absolutely. After landing we travelled down muddy tracks to the foremost frontline. I noticed again and again how tired officers and men, coated in the filth of the unmade roads, reacted as if electrified when Hitler appeared near them. As he came up with a silent smile, right where the bullets were whistling, this was the last place they had expected to see him. Yet it was so, and nobody, whether at the front or in the homeland, could be certain that Hitler would not suddenly pop up just where they were standing. In peacetime he had used travel specifically as a tool of leadership. He had withdrawn willingly from the immediate confrontations with his ministers and Party functionaries and 'reigned' through his personal adjutants. During the war, as warlord and strategist, he travelled for other reasons. Since he thought he could not trust his own military commanders, he wanted to keep his finger on the pulse of events so as to make effective decisions at close quarters.

Now it was different to the 'good times' in which the war-god Hitler had been reared. He spoke amongst his closest circle increasingly of the past. He fled into history and compared it to the present, as he wanted it to be. Considering his world-view, it was no wonder that Great Britain was generally at the centre of his ramblings. He accused Churchill, 'stiff-necked and politically stupid', of having disappointed him. He had offered Churchill the opportunity of resuming the world political role that the great Pitt had pursued in an earlier century. Pitt's policies, and Churchill must have been aware of them, would have held the world in equilibrium, which Churchill – contrary to Pitt – had failed to do by making common cause with France. 'The things I have done or neglected to do so as not to injure British pride,' Hitler exclaimed at the beginning of 1945. He accused Churchill of having succumbed to Jewish influences, whose exponents and originators preferred to let the empire fall apart rather than arrange an accord with 'Nazi Germany'. He, Hitler, placed no blame upon himself for failing to take certain measures or, as he admitted, for having made treaties which – as for example the alliance with Stalin – finally proved a major disadvantage for the Reich. He also criticised himself for being 'too good' after seizing power and not having been ruthless enough in ridding himself of those upon whose loyalty he had not been able to rely.

In connection with British policies, Hitler was convinced that the British might have been prepared to accept a 'pseudo anti-semitism', but his own more rigorous brand of anti-semitism was probably too much for 'the cousins over there'. If Pitt had been prime minister instead of Churchill, by the latest at the beginning of 1945 Britain would probably have 'seized the chance' to end the war, he went on, and he blamed the British for having deliberately started it in 1939. I noticed that Hitler no longer spoke of victory, and if nobody else was about he would talk of us 'having to keep this struggle going to the death'.

Looking at the portrait of Frederick the Great, Hitler said one night: 'In the winter of 1762 he was ready to give up and take poison if he did not succeed in changing his fortunes in war. The unexpected death of the Russian tsarina, Elizabeth, put a stop to his thoughts of suicide.' There never was any such thing as a totally hopeless situation in history, and we could claim it as a victory if we succeeded 'in simply surviving' with an independent existence. I never repeated anywhere what I heard issue from Hitler's lips in the first weeks and months of 1945. Hitler knew this, and in the night-time hours gave me a vision of a past, present and future which I, rooted in realities of a quite different structure, misunderstood in astonishment. In those weeks , in which Martin Bormann wrote down what Hitler had explained to him, it seemed to me at times that Hitler was attempting to escape in these conversations from the reality which had long overtaken him.

Occasionally when we were alone he spoke of our 'future' and painted it in very different colours to how it turned out, and only later did I discover what we Germans ought to have known earlier. Just as in the last hours of his life Hitler still saw the historical duty of the German people to be biological anti-semitism, even in the future, so convinced was he to his last breath that 'our future lay only in the east' and that it was so important for 'our surplus births' to be channelled there. Even today I ask myself now and again how I was able to believe what Hitler said and taught. The Red Army was almost at the gates of the Reich capital, yet I allowed myself to be persuaded: 'We will come out of it, even if plucked of our feathers.' We came out of it all right, but not in the manner I was daring to hope under the spell of Hitler's powers of persuasion in April 1945.

I was not an intellectual. Like most of my comrades, I had read neither *Mein Kampf* nor any other National Socialist literature and I knew Hitler's world-view only from hearsay. What gave me unshakable faith and confidence came from other experiences. One of these was that for years the Führer had found a way to achieve what he had aimed for and predicted despite all obstacles. Screened in his immediate circle against all negative ideas which might be circulating elsewhere, I was blind to the reality. Unlikely as it may sound, I saw how Hitler held the levers of powers in his hands, and I was often there as he occupied himself with them, but where he was steering us was something I could not see.

What gave me pause for thought occasionally was the fact that Hitler did not lead and govern as the people thought. To a great extent he gave ministers, Reichsleiters, Gauleiters and governor-generals a free hand, and not seldom they turned on each other tooth and nail. I saw that kind of thing almost daily, but knowing that the Führer, despite the so-called 'Darwinism of the Offices' always held the true reins of power in principle, kept my doubts at bay. However, I did begin to listen attentively when he began his monologues on history and politics.

Nudging me in this direction was a remark by Hitler that before the war it would not have been difficult to have won over General Franco for war on the German side. Ribbentrop's occasional whispered confidences that unfortunately the attempt to draw

Franco into the war had not succeeded, seemed to conflict with Hitler's statement that Franco had wanted nothing more than to join with Hitler and Mussolini as victors. In the presence of Bormann, Hitler declared that after mature deliberation he had finally decided against trying to convince the Caudillo to make common cause. The prospect of having to defend the Atlantic coast from Cadiz to San Sebastian while a new civil war, fanned by the British, raged inland, had – together with other burdens – seemed to counsel restraint. 'Franco', Hitler said, 'deceived me. Had I known the true state of affairs I would not have used our aircraft to return to the Spanish aristocracy and the Catholic Church their mediaeval rights.'

I now began to listen to, and systematically study, similar 'confessions' and explanations. Thus I only made myself familiar with the National Socialist world-view fwhen the founder of the ideology was at the edge of his grave, but at least I heard it from the 'prophet' himself. For him, whom I watched read very, very much over my ten years in his company, past and future represented themselves at the beginning of 1945 in the following manner: The great material battles of the First World War had exhausted the political power structures of Europe. This led to a concentration of political power in blocs, in which the growing might of the United States, the Soviet Union and Japan could no longer be ignored. Britain, which together with the Third Reich could have been the dominant world power, lost this opportunity as a result of Churchill's policies. If at the latest by the spring of 1941 Great Britain had joined with Hitler's Germany, a strong bloc would have emerged in Europe, under German leadership, in which France and Italy would have been obliged to abandon their interests in north Africa and the Near East and renounce a world foreign policy. Britain, freed of power struggles on the continent, would have been able to devote itself to its empire, while the Reich, forced to win living space by conquest but no longer having to fear war on two fronts, would have been able to destroy Bolshevism and 'secure' the indispensable territories in the east for the German people. That this could not be realised was Britain's fault and the people of the island kingdom which – in contrast to Germany – had not been actually forced to fight by anyone, would vegetate and finally starve 'on their damned island'. After Hitler saw that he could not terminate the war by an invasion of England, he said he had then decided to order the attack on Russia and accept a war on two fronts which until then he had always warned against. As Germany would have no prospect of winning a defensive war to repel a Russian attack, which would certainly have come some day, there had been only one solution – attack them first. That he had given the order for the military preparations on the day when Molotov left for Moscow after talks with Hitler and Ribbentrop, as he expressly emphasised, I judged to be proof of his political far-sightedness.

In captivity I said nothing about these statements of Hitler's regarding the Russians. Even if I had believed it all, it would have served no useful purpose. On the other hand, it was different with Hitler's accusations against the foreign minister and certain military leaders that they had conducted a totally false French policy. He implied that Ribbentrop and his advisers had pursued a foreign policy independent of his will. Often enough I had been present when he gave Ribbentrop binding instructions respecting the policy in France and towards France. Now, after everything had gone awry, he spoke balefully of 'our geniuses in the Wilhelm-Strasse', of the 'military men of the old school' and 'village Junkers from east of the Elbe', all of whom had failed to understand that twentieth-century France had the face of a whore and that only one policy applied: the policy of ice-cold distrust.

What seemed to me most worthy of note was what Hitler said about the Jews in the last days and weeks of his life. Contrary to previous statements in speeches and so on, in which he had always spoken of the 'Jewish race', he now said that from the genetic and anthropological point of view there was no actual Jewish race, and that one spoke of a Jewish race only for 'convenience in discussion'. Jewry was not a special race, but a spiritual community bound not least to the fate of those of its members persecuted since time immemorial. This interpretation had its roots in the idea that Jewry, whose existence he considered a 'sad victory of spirit over flesh', had been responsible for all the evils in history and for which one day it must atone. He himself had made a start in wiping out Jewry, from which humanity had to be 'liberated'. There could therefore be no talk of a fundamental deviation from his doctrine. This left me none the wiser.

My blind faith in Hitler and his vaunted abilities caused me to overlook many things initially, mainly because of the speed with which everything happened. Not until later when everything was over and I reviewed the momentous events of the past in my mind's eye did I become aware of certain details, which particularly during the war should have made me more pensive. Hitler always knew, at least in outline, what he intended, but he gave himself time to make his decisions even when they were urgent. Although he often spoke of 'dirty tricks' which he feared from the enemy, he let things run. He ignored the occasional cautious pressure by the military commanders, whom he accused of being *laurig*, shy of making decisions and happy to procrastinate. Often I had the impression that he would have liked to have had military commanders who led their troops 'sword in hand', as he once said. So far as I could see there was nobody in the army staff who fitted the bill. During the war much would have advanced faster and turned out better if somebody knowledgeable and decisive whom he respected had constantly urged Hitler to act now rather than delay his decision until it was really too late. Hitler, who – contrary to all opposing assertions – knew his weaknesses as a leader – changed nothing in this respect and limited himself to retrospective admissions: 'If only I had done that sooner . . .'

What 'one' could do and achieve under Hitler was demonstrated impressively by Martin Bormann. Never do I recall Hitler 'calling someone back' because he had stepped out of his jurisdiction. In the main he would outline what he wanted done very vaguely and would willingly allow somebody to take over once the thing was in motion and he had imagined it 'in principle'. It would be his preference to give at least two people or departments the same task and watch who did it better, or outdid the competitor. That this policy was bound to lead to unnecessary friction, delays, duplication of work and differing results was obvious. In my ten years with Hitler I experienced at first hand that what Hitler did not like to do himself he would demand of others. He recognised his own defects and did not want to see them in others. A decisive fault of his in my opinion was that he did not admit this so openly as might be expected. Thus I saw military commanders leaving situation conferences pensive, and even shaking their heads, which would have been unnecessary if . . . but this 'if' was part of Hitler's style of leadership. As the military men in commanding positions knew me and would often discuss matters with me, their opinions were not always carefully hidden. The result was that often they criticised the 'irresoluteness of the Führer' and even seemed in certain situations to flounder, like children disappointed by Santa Claus.

That Hitler was disappointed equally by them after such conferences they would be probably unaware. 'I would get from them', he would growl, 'nothing but mediocrity. They are strangers to great initiatives.' Once after leaving a situation conference in depression he said: 'If I knew a suitable major, I would make him chief of the general staff on the spot', and then after a short pause, 'but where should I find him? Where would I take him from?' I saw and heard the Führer, and I saw and heard the military. They were simply two 'positions' that did not coincide.

*

Hitler's constantly worsening health and fear of dying before he had 'completed his work' were major influences on his decision-making. From 1936 to 1942 he was often not only sick but also often so sick that he believed himself at death's door. In 1943 came the transition. Overnight he became an old man physically, who from the end of 1944 moved without agility – bent both forwards and sideways. If he wanted to sit, a chair had to be placed for him. His left arm and leg had trembled since the defeat at Stalingrad. 'Nervous pains' as he called his jitters, problems with his alimentary system, heartburn and flatulence plagued him so oppressively that he would often have difficulty in hiding it from the military men. Often he would just sit there with painfully distorted features.

What I could not understand was the source of the enormous energy he radiated and transmitted to others. The sorry picture he made and his reactions did not synchronise. If a stranger had seen him for the first time, he would have felt sorry for him while Hitler sat there silently. Yet though exhausted and washed out physically, his mind was aggressive, watchful and reacted lightning fast. If adjutants or military men brought statistics or reports he needed only to glance through them to know them by heart if necessary. His incredible memory did not desert him in this phase of his life. Mentally he was still a giant who overshadowed all around him. He knew this, but remained in a state of hectic watchfulness, suspicious of almost everybody.

Besides Dönitz, Goebbels, Bormann and ourselves, that is to say, his closest circle, Hitler trusted nobody. Everywhere he detected danger and obstruction. As events proved, this fear was not groundless. Even Himmler had negotiated 'with the enemy' against Hitler's wishes, as became clear at the end. Under no circumstances whatever, even less than in previous years, did Hitler want to be bed-ridden now. He clenched his teeth, his broken body under a great coat and tried to present the image of a physically intact Führer. He ignored the continual urgings of Goebbels 'to finally make another great speech', but allowed soldiers from the front to 'visit' him.

Still convinced of his extraordinary suggestive power, Hitler did not avoid confrontations which might have overwhelmed him in his pitiable condition; on the contrary, he went out of his way to seek them out. For me it was a phenomenon difficult to understand: generals, officers, NCOs and men who knew the athletic-looking Führer from photos were suddenly confronted by a man who bore no resemblance to the picture-book Hitler, yet they departed from him fascinated, having forgotten momentarily the image they had had before. Military officers arriving from the front angry, disappointed, aggressive and determined 'to finally put him straight and describe what it really looks like at the front' left his presence changed men. 'The Führer has explained', they beamed without exception. The Führer had put *them* straight. Only very few of them noticed how burned out the volcano was which had forced their reorientatation.

A theory has been cultivated in certain circles, similar to the 'stab in the back' legend, that in the final phase of his life the Führer was no longer master of his senses – that this is the only way by which the catastrophic end of the Third Reich can be explained. This is a fable. Up to that final moment when he took his pistol, held it to his right temple and pulled the trigger, he was Adolf Hitler, one hundred per cent *compos mentis*. Thus all references to the contrary which have appeared since then are superfluous.

To my recollection, other events after Hitler's last birthday are not as retold. On 19 April 1945, Johann Rattenhuber, head of the RSD, showed me an SD report stating that one of the Führer's orderlies would attempt to murder him on 20 April, his birthday. The assassin would be a man who wore civilian clothing and had a hand wound received at the front. Nobody fitted this description. Orderlies in civilian attire had only been seen on Obersalzberg before the war. Possibly this was one of the many false alarms generated by Fegelein, whom we never used to take seriously. The report might possibly have given me cause to be specially cautious on the day itself, but it was unnecessary, for I could not be more attentive and watchful than I was at any time in the execution of my duty, and the Führer, who trusted me blindly, knew that. He said once: 'Linge, when you sit or stand behind me, I feel more secure than if one of the Obergruppenführers were to stand in your place.'

On previous occasions, Führer birthdays had been celebrated as follows: Hitler's personal staff appeared at midnight on 19 April and were the first to offer their congratulations after myself, for I had to tell Hitler that the staff had come for that purpose. In 1945 everything was different. Hitler had told me beforehand that he would not receive well-wishers, which I should communicate to them. There was nothing for people to congratulate him about. Nevertheless towards midnight on 19 April SS-Gruppenführer Hermann Fegelein, Julius Schaub (Hitler's personal adjutant), naval adjutant Albrecht, adjutant Otto Günsche (the chief of the Reich Chancellery adjutancy), diplomat Walther Hewel (representing Ribbentrop at FHQ) and Werner Lorenz (representing the Reich press chief) assembled in the ante-chamber of chief adjutant General Wilhelm Burgdorf.

After informing Hitler of this he gave me a tired and depressed look. I had to tell the arrivals that the Führer had no time to receive them. Shortly afterwards Fegelein, who was married to Eva Braun's sister Gretl and was on very familiar terms with Eva, used these 'relationships' in an attempt to convince his sister-in-law to get Hitler to receive the party of well-wishers who were intent on remaining where they were until able to offer their congratulations. Eva succeeded, and very reluctantly Hitler rose and shuffled to the ante-chamber, shoulders drooping, so that everybody could say individually: 'I congratulate you' Then they saw his back as he retreated.

Hans Baur (Hitler's chief pilot), Betz (his second pilot), Rattenhuber (RSD commander), Peter Högl (RSD deputy commander), and Franz Schaedle (head of the SS bodyguard at the

Reich Chancellery), who also wanted to offer their birthday wishes, missed their chance, although in the early hours they came across Hitler on his way from his room to the military conference room and in passing he shook the hand of every man. The situation conference lasted only a brief time, and Eva Braun came to his study where both took tea and wished to be alone. The birthday fitted the situation.

Scarcely had Hitler and Eva Braun retired – it was about nine in the morning – than General Burgdorf arrived and, wringing his hands, begged me to 'wake the Führer for God's sake' so that he, Burgdorf, could relay to him a very important message from the front. I did so. Hitler, who rose at once but neither dressed nor left his bedroom, came only to the door and asked from the other side of it: 'What's up, Burgdorf?'. The general was standing next to me, and reported that Russian divisions had broken through between Guben and Forst, counterattacks had already been made and the commander of the German forces had been shot for 'failing in his defence of the front sector'. Hitler replied: 'Linge, I have not slept yet. Wake me an hour later than usual at 1400 hours.' I obeyed his order, after which he had breakfast and had me trickle some cocaine drops into his right eye. We did not talk. He wanted me to bring him Wolf, his favourite puppy from the litter of his German Shepherd Blondi, and he played with the puppy until lunch, which he ate alone with Eva Braun and the female secretaries. He had now totally isolated himself and wanted to see nobody but Eva and me.

Hitler could not flee the present entirely. Towards 1500 hours, Hitler Youth deputies under Arthur Axmann's leadership, officers of army group Mitte, the FHQ commandant, the chief of the Führer's guard company, one of Bormann's colleagues and some SS men at the Reich Chancellery bunker exit also came to congratulate him. Hitler, wearing a field-grey greatcoat, drew up the collar and in company of naval adjutant Karl-Jesko von Puttkamer and myself proceeded to the waiting well-wishers who at our appearance came silently to attention and gave the Hitler salute.

In the park, at the door to the Winter Garden, were Himmler, Bormann, Burgdorf, Fegelein, Hewel, Lorenz, Hitler's doctors Morell and Stumpfegger, Schaub, Albert Bormann, Albrecht, Willi Johannmeier, Luftwaffe adjutant Nikolaus von Below and Günsche. Himmler went up to Hitler and congratulated him. Hitler offered his hand, but I saw from the handshake that his mind was clearly elsewhere. After Hitler – tired, bent, of greyish pallor and weak – shuffled back from the 'front' having received their birthday wishes, he allowed them to form into a semi-circle before him in order to receive his message. What they heard from his lips did nothing to 'release' them from the conviction, having regard to the depressing military situation, that total defeat was imminent even though Hitler still attempted to foster the opposite impression.

Since the daily conference had been scheduled for 1600 hours, Himmler, Bormann, Burgdorf, Fegelein and the adjutants followed the Führer into the bunker, which he would never leave again alive. Then came Göring, Ribbentrop, Dönitz, Keitel and Jodl, whom I announced individually and escorted to Hitler to offer their congratulations. Nobody spoke of the catastrophic finale, each assured Hitler of his faithfulness unto death. After this, which had not improved Hitler's mood, he thanked those present in the ante-chamber for their best wishes and promises and asked the chief of the general staff, Hans Krebs, how the situation on the Oder river was developing. Göring, with whom Hitler had had a brief conversation in his study, left Berlin again.

Two days later on the afternoon of 22 April, Hitler stated during a situation conference that he was going to remain in Berlin. We, who until then had been hoping that he would soon transfer his HQ to the so-called Alpine Redoubt, were one disappointment richer. Above all for Martin Bormann, who had already made all kinds of preparations, this was a hammer blow. He had already painted himself a picture of how it would be 'in the Bavarian Alps'. Goebbels was dreaming of the heroic end in Berlin and described Hitler's decision as an historic act.

What brought Hitler to this decision is hard to say. Perhaps it had something to do with the failure to obey orders by SS-General Felix Steiner, whom Hitler had told on 21 April to ward off the Russians from the Reich capital at all costs using Luftwaffe support. Because there were hardly any German aircraft available and the units mentioned by the Führer existed partially in name only, Steiner had preferred to head West and lead his troops into US captivity. When Hitler heard this he was beside himself with rage, accusing Steiner of treason, of lying, of cowardice and of failure. He had no more orders for the Wehrmacht, he declared. Now Göring, who was better suited to negotiating with the enemy than he was, should see how he got on with that. Everybody who did not absolutely need to see Hitler chose to avoid him. I had no choice, of course, but towards me he forced himself to be 'calm'.

'There you have it, Linge', he growled, 'even the SS goes behind my back and deceives me wherever they can. Now I shall remain in Berlin and die here. As I am too infirm to carry a weapon I shall take my own life, as is fitting for the commandant of a redoubt.' Even Bormann's attempt of 23 April to win over Speer, whom he had treated recently with such disdain, failed. Speer, who visited Hitler that day to take his leave of him, had his own worries. I do not know if he recommended that Hitler should vacate Berlin for I was not in attendance during their last conversation together. Bormann had intercepted Speer at the door and asked him in a quite friendly manner to do something he had never managed to achieve himself before – 'change the Führer's mind'. All such efforts to get Hitler to leave Berlin fell on deaf ears.

Some optimists began to see a surreal purpose in Hitler's remaining in Berlin, thinking that he could still achieve some kind of victory from there. They were all too ready to see in every favourable momentary flicker of light a positive and decisive turn in Germany's fortunes. On 26 April 1945, for example, Ferdinand Schörner, operating from Bohemia, had won ground unexpectedly in the direction of Berlin. Walther Wenck's army broke through to Potsdam. The Russian encirclement of Berlin seemed threatened from the north. Hitler radiated confidence. But it was only a brief flare. It died down, our panzers turned away and headed northwards, away from Berlin. Apathy followed the short period of euphoria. Hitler's female secretaries requested poison ampoules from the Boss 'for the ultimate eventuality'. Hewel did so too. SS-General Hermann Fegelein, Himmler's liaison officer to Hitler, disappeared suddenly.

Hitler, already infuriated and crestfallen at the Reuters report he had just received about Himmler's attempt to negotiate peace with the Western Allies, suspected 'treasonable circumstances'. 'Where is Fegelein?' roared Bormann, 'where is the guy?' SS-Obersturmbannführer Kempka, Hitler's driver, replied that on Fegelein's orders he had released to him the last two service vehicles at the Reich Chancellery 'for a service task'. These vehicles had returned, but without Fegelein, who had placed himself near the Kurfürstendamm for some kind of 'information-gathering exercise'. When Fegelein's adjutant reported back to the bunker, he stated that Fegelein had gone to his private flat and dressed in civilian clothing. The adjutant had been ordered to do the same, the purpose of this being 'to allow the Russians to roll over us and then we will make our way through to Himmler'. The adjutant had not been prepared to go along with the idea. For Bormann, Hitler, and everybody else it was clear: Fegelein was a coward and traitor who was fleeing before the enemy. Disguised as a civilian, he had attempted to sneak away even though he was not just an SS-general but also Eva Braun's brother-in-law. On 27 April the RSD went to his flat and found him with a woman. She was not Eva Braun's sister Gretl, his wife, but an unknown female.[2] With 100,000 RM, gold and jewellery ready

2 According to Christa Schroeder: *Er War Mein Chef*, Herbig 1985, pp.371–2, Fegelein was arrested by SS Obersturmbannführer Peter Högl of the RSD in his

packed, he had been hoping to leave Berlin unnoticed after failing to convince Eva Braun in a telephone conversation the previous day that she should also leave the Reich capital as soon as she could.

Returned under armed guard he made a poor impression: wearing gloves, a leather coat and a sporty hat he looked like a Kurfürstendamm 'dandy'. On Hitler's order he was arraigned immediately before a court-martial and sentenced to death for treason. Eva Braun, though clearly fighting an internal struggle, would not enter a plea for mercy for her brother-in-law even though Hitler indicated that he would commute the sentence on the highly decorated SS-Obergruppenführer to 'atonement at the front'. Towards midnight an SS squad awaited Fegelein in the Reich Chancellery Ehrenhof. He remained impassive as the sentence of the court martial was read out.

Soon after the execution Hitler called me into his study. After I had entered and reported myself in military fashion he said without any preamble: 'I would like to release you to your family.' I now did something I had never done before by interrupting him to declare: 'Mein Führer, I have been with you in good times, and I am staying with you also in the bad.' Hitler looked at me calmly and said only: 'I did not expect anything else from you.' Then, standing at his writing desk, he went on: 'I have another personal job for you. What I must do now is what I have ordered every commander at every redoubt to do: hold out to the death. This order is also binding on myself, since I feel that I am here as the commandant of Berlin. You should hold in readiness woollen blankets in my bedroom and enough petrol for two cremations. I am going to shoot myself here together with Eva Braun. You will wrap our bodies in woollen blankets, carry them up to the garden, and there burn them.' I stood paralysed. 'Jawohl, mein Führer,' I stuttered, trembling. I could find nothing else to say.

---

flat at Bleibtreu-Strasse 10–11. He was in the company of a red-haired woman who escaped by means of a ruse before her identity could be ascertained.

Swiftly, knees feeling as though they were about to collapse under me, I left Hitler. Things were going round and round in my head. I went to my friends Högl and Schaedle and told them what I had been ordered, and asked for their help in the task. Then I called for Hitler's driver, Kempka, to place some canisters of petrol near the bunker exit. 'Petrol?' he asked doubtfully. I said I would explain to him in private what the fuel was for. Then I had a couple of glasses of schnapps to help me get over the shock.

Once I could think clearly again I asked myself how I would have reacted if he had asked me to shoot Eva Braun and himself personally. I have literally no idea what my decision would have been. At the tea session in the bunker next evening the conversation was morbid. The principal topic was 'what is the most favoured way to die by your own hand?' Shooting and poison were generally considered the 'most acceptable' means of suicide. Each of us thought over the question of how we would prefer to put an end to ourselves or at least it looked as if everybody were considering the question.

The often-alleged assertions that there was drunken debauchery, indiscipline and 'mutiny' in the Führer-bunker are all nonsense. While Hitler lived, everything proceeded precisely as before. There was a bunker below the New Reich Chancellery containing quarters for everybody not required to live in the Führer-bunker, and what went on there I have no idea. Naturally we took alcohol, but still in moderation. Now as before we paid the usual heed to Hitler, whose mere presence alone would have stifled at inception any disobedience or indiscipline. Only on the last night of his life, when additional mattresses were laid in the situation room for female secretaries or other people from his immediate circle who might be required to stay overnight, did one have to step over a secretary or some other worker sleeping on the floor. Hitler and Eva Braun saw hardly any of this. The much-hawked description of Hitler, propping himself up on a walking stick, stepping with difficulty over drunken adjutants and functionaries on the floor who failed to show him any kind of respect, has no basis in fact.

I had imagined the Führer's marriage differently in earlier years. Now when it was finally held there was probably nobody who was not disappointed. There were few people present. When registrar Walter Wagner, clad in Volkssturm uniform, arrived shortly before one o'clock on the morning of 29 April, everything was ready. Hitler had had the situation conference room set up for the ceremony. At one side of the table were four chairs, one each for Hitler, Eva Braun and the witnesses Goebbels and Bormann. After the witnesses had been advised as to their role they waited with the 'guests'. Registrar Wagner, as excited as Eva Braun, had a two-page typed document from which he requested the contracting parties to declare that they were of Aryan origin and free of any hereditary disease which would present an impediment to the marriage. Then Wagner said in trembling tones: 'I come now to the solemn act of the marriage. In the presence of the witnesses I ask you, mein Führer Adolf Hitler, if you are so willed as to enter wedlock with Fräulein Eva Braun. In this case I request that you answer with 'Yes'. Hitler did this, and then Eva Braun did so, after Wagner had continued: 'Now I ask you, Fräulein Eva Braun, if you are so willed as to enter wedlock with our Führer Adolf Hitler.' After a concluding paragraph and the signature of the Hitler, Eva Hitler, Goebbels, Bormann and registrar Wagner to the certificate, the ceremony was over.

Hitler and his bride accepted our best wishes. After they retired ninety minutes later, we celebrated with the Goebbels family, Bormann. Burgdorf, Hewel, Axmann, von Below, Hitler's secretary Gerda Christian and the personal adjutant. Champagne, sandwiches and tea were served in a fitting atmosphere.

In captivity the Russians asked me why Hitler had married on the last full day of his life. In this they saw proof for their theory that Hitler was a typical middle-class citizen who required everything to be 'rubber-stamped and official' for it to have any validity: 'You Germans', an NKVD intelligence officer remarked to me disparagingly in this connection, 'are only revolutionaries if you have a piece of paper authorising it.' There was no point in explaining to him that Hitler's decision to marry Eva Braun 'properly' resulted from quite different motives. It is certain that the ceremony and its consequences meant nothing at all to him. He merely wanted to fulfil Eva's wish that after coming to him in Berlin, she should die at his side as his lawful wife. In principle this is put another way in his Last Will and Testament of 29 April 1945:

> . . . Since I believed during the years of struggle that I should not accept the responsibility of marriage, I have decided before ending my earthly span to make that girl my wife who, after long years of loyal friendship, came of her own free will into an almost besieged city in order to share her fate with mine. It is her wish that she should accompany me into death as my wife. Death will replace for us that of which my work robbed us both in the service of my people.[3]

Eva Hitler's composure after her marriage proved Hitler right. For a while she seemed to have forgotten the catastrophe and her environment. When I saw her afterwards, instead of addressing her as *gnädiges Fräulein* as I always had done, or *gnädige Frau* as she now was, I preferred the emphatic 'Frau Hitler'. Her eyes lit up. She gave me a happy smile and for a moment laid her hand on my forearm. Eva Hitler. She had dreamed of this for more than ten years. Instinctively I thought of what Kurt Tucholsky had written, according to which one gets one's heart's desire, but always a day too late and always a size too small. This seemed coined for Eva Hitler, who went off to bed with her husband after drinks. We, 'the most intimate circle', stayed behind and celebrated the marriage

3 Werner Maser, *Hitlers Briefe und Notizen, Sein Weltbild in Handschriftlichen Dokumenten*, Düsseldorf 1973, p.212.

'deep below the ground' while the Russian artillery churned up the parkland around the Reich Chancellery.

Chapter 17

Hitler's Suicide

THE NEXT DAY, 30 April 1945, I went to Hitler in the early morning. He was opening the door as I arrived. He had lain on the bed fully dressed and awake as he had done the night before. While Bormann, Krebs and Burgdorf kept loaded pistols within reach, safety catches off, and dozed on sofas near his door, and the female secretaries made themselves as comfortable as possible while awaiting the events that must soon come (at any moment the Russians could reach the bunker entrance), he signalled to me to accompany him, finger to his lips, indicating I should be careful not to disturb the sleeping figures. We went to the telephone exchange, where Hitler rang the commandant, who told him that the defence of Berlin had already collapsed. The ring which the Russians had laid around the city could no longer be penetrated, and there was now no hope of relief. Arthur Axmann did offer to 'bring the Führer out of Berlin' using about 200 Hitler Youth volunteers and a panzer, but Hitler declined, murmuring quietly,: 'That is no longer an option, I am remaining here!'

The 'hour of truth' had come. Firstly, however, there was a last midday meal to be taken together. Hitler delivered a monologue about the future. The immediate postwar world would not have a good word to say for him, he said: the enemy would savour its triumph, and the German people would face very difficult times. Even we, his intimate circle, would soon experience things that we could not imagine. But he trusted to 'the later histories' to 'treat him justly'. They would recognise that he had only wanted the very best for Germany. Not until after my release from captivity did I understand what he meant when he said: 'You will soon experience things' that 'you cannot imagine'.

After the meal Eva Hitler came to me to take her leave. Pale, having remained awake all night but careful to maintain her composure, she thanked me for 'everything you have done for the Führer'. With a sad look she begged me at the finish: 'Should you meet my sister Gretl, do not tell her how her husband, Hermann Fegelein, met his death.' I never saw Gretl Fegelein again. Next she went to Frau Goebbels while Hitler retired to his study. Magda Goebbels wanted another 'personal conversation with the Führer', as Günsche told me. I approached Hitler and he allowed her to come. They were alone for a while. When I entered, Hitler was thanking her for her commitment and services. He asked me to remove the gold Party badge from one of his uniforms and pinned it on her in 'especial recognition'. Immediately after this Hitler and I went into the common room where Goebbels appeared and begged Hitler briefly to allow the Hitler Youth to take him out of Berlin. Hitler responded brusquely: 'Doctor, you know my decision. There is no change! You can of course leave Berlin with your family.' Goebbels, standing proudly, replied that he would not do so. Like the Führer he intended to stay in Berlin – and die there. At that Hitler gave Goebbels his hand and, leaning on me, returned to his room.

Immediately afterwards followed the last personal goodbyes. Flugkapitän Baur and SS-Sturmbannführer Otto Günsche came, two men who had dedicated their lives to Hitler. My mouth was dry. Soon I would have to carry out my last duty. Anxiously I gazed at the man whom I had served devotedly for more than ten years. He stood stooped, the hank of hair, as always, across the pale forehead. He had become grey. He looked at me with tired eyes and said he would now retire. It was 1515 hours. I asked for his orders for the last time. Outwardly calm and in a quiet voice, as if he were sending me into the garden to fetch something, he said: 'Linge, I am going to shoot myself now. You know what you have to do. I have given the order for the break-out. Attach yourself to one of the groups and try to get through to the west.' To my question what we should fight for now, he answered: 'For the Coming Man'. I saluted. Hitler took two or three tired steps towards me and offered his hand. Then for the last time in his life he raised his right arm in the Hitler salute. A ghostly scene. I turned on my heel, closed the door and went to the bunker exit where the SS bodyguard was sitting around.

As I assumed that Hitler would put an end to his life at any moment I did not stay there long, but returned to the ante-room. I smelt the gas from a discharged firearm. Thus it had come to pass. Although I was beyond surprises, everything in me resisted opening the door and entering alone. I went to the map room where a number of people were gathered around Martin Bormann. What they were discussing I have no idea. They had no knowledge of what had happened. I gave Bormann a signal and asked him to come with me to Hitler's room, which he did.

I opened the door and went in, Bormann following me. He turned white as chalk and stared at me helplessly. Adolf Hitler and Eva Braun were seated on the sofa. Both were dead. Hitler had shot himself in the right temple with his 7.65-mm pistol. This weapon, and his 6.35-mm pistol which he had kept in reserve in the event that the larger gun misfired, lay near his feet on the floor. His head was inclined a little towards the wall. Blood had spattered on the carpet near the sofa. To his right beside him sat his wife. She had drawn up her legs on the sofa. Her contorted face betrayed how she had died. Cyanide poisoning. Its 'bite' was marked in her features. The small box in which the capsule had been kept lay on the table. I pushed it aside to give myself room.

While Bormann went outside to fetch help to remove the bodies, I spread out the blankets, laid the cadavers on them and wrapped them round. It did not strike me until later, when the Russians asked me about it, that I did not see Hitler's face closely, and I was unable to say what damage the bullet had inflicted to his head. My main aim was to finish and get away. Eva Hitler was carried out first. Erich Kempka lifted her up but then replaced her on the floor so that Günsche could take over because he found it awkward to carry her alone. Bormann picked her up in his arms and brought the body out of the room where Kempka took over again because he did not like the idea of the man she had despised in life carrying her now 'to the grave'.

I reached below Hitler's head, two officers from his SS bodyguard lifted the body, wrapped in a grey blanket, and we carried him out. Immediately in front of the bunker door, in the Reich Chancellery garden, his body was laid next to Eva's in a small depression where gasoline was poured over the cadavers and an attempt was made to set light to them. At first this proved impossible. As a result of the various fires in the parkland there was a fierce wind circulating which smothered our attempts to set the bodies alight from a few metres' distance. Because of the relentless Russian artillery fire we could not approach the bodies and ignite the petrol with a match. I returned to the bunker and made a thick spill from some signal papers. Bormann lit it and I threw it onto Hitler's petrol-soaked body which caught fire immediately. Standing at the bunker entrance we, the last witnesses – Bormann, Goebbels, Stumpfegger, Günsche, Kempka and I – raised our hands for a last Hitler salute. Then we withdrew into the bunker.*

---

* There are many inconsistencies regarding Hitler's suicide between the accounts of the three eye-witnesses to survive the war. These witnesses were: SS Obersturmbannführer Erich Kempka (manager of the Reich Chancellery vehicle pool and Hitler's personal driver), SS Sturmbannführer Otto Günsche (Hitler's adjutant), and SS Hauptsturmführer Heinz Linge (the author). These three SS officers cannot even agree the time of day when the suicide occurred. Günsche and Linge stated 'about 1530'; Kempka said it was 'well before two o'clock'. Kempka, responsible for supplying the petrol, also stated that the bodies were burning between 1400 and 1930 hours. Hitler is supposed to have shot himself in the head with a Walter PPK 7.65-mm pistol. Nobody witnessed this. Kempka says that

Since Hitler had given me the additional task of burning everything that remained of him, I had no time to concern myself with the bodies. These were still burning towards 1930 hours. I destroyed the bloodstained carpet, Hitler's uniforms, his medicines, documents etc. While I was doing this a squad under the command of an SS bodyguard officer buried the carbonised bodies in a shell crater. Everything had to be done quickly and secretly, for if the fighting troops in the Reich Chancellery and defending the government district knew what had transpired they were likely to abandon their weapons. I realised at the time that that must not happen, because Hitler had arranged for a government to continue the struggle. Bormann, Goebbels and a few military men went to the situation conference room to decide how to proceed in Hitler's absence.

When I met the new Reich Chancellor Dr Joseph Goebbels next morning, he stopped me to ask why I had not made Hitler change his mind about committing suicide. 'Herr Doktor, if you were unable to do it, how should I?' I replied. 'Yes, Linge', he admitted, 'last night I also intended shooting myself, but it is a very difficult thing to do. I simply could not do it.'

Now we sat in the bunker and hoped in vain that the Russians would agree to the terms that General Krebs offered them on Dr Goebbels's behalf on the morning of 1 May 1945. In Russian

---

Günsche told him the shot had been heard by Günsche, Linge and Bormann, and all three entered the Führer's room together; Linge said he did not hear the shot but smelt the gas from the discharge and went to find Bormann. Kempka saw the dead Hitler's head 'uncovered from the nose upward: he thought it worth mentioning the greying hair but did not describe any dried blood in the hair or any head wound, while Linge was 'unable to describe any damage to Hitler's head' because he did not look. Günsche was silent on the matter. Therefore, if there was a head wound, none of the three surviving witnesses saw it.

The only thing they do all agree on is that Günsche and Kempka brought up the body of Eva Hitler. However, Linge said the body of Eva was carried up first, while Kempka said that Hitler's body went up first. Linge stated that he carried up Hitler's body with the help of two SS bodyguards; Kempka said that Hitler was carried up by Linge and Dr Stumpfegger. (TN)

captivity Soviet officers told me why the meeting between Krebs and the Russian generals Chuikov and Sokolovski had a negative outcome. The Russians wanted the capitulation. Krebs did not have this authority. The protocol of the negotiations compiled by the Russians reads:

Krebs (K): I will speak completely frankly. You are the first non-Germans to whom I pass the news that Hitler committed suicide on 30 April.

Chuikov (Ch): We know that.

K: Following the Führer's testament . . . (he reads Hitler's testament and an official declaration by Dr Goebbels). Aim of this declaration is a favourable solution for the peoples who had the greatest losses in human lives in this war. The document can be given to your commander.

Ch: Are we talking here about Berlin or all Germany?

K: I am empowered to speak for all German armies. Empowered by Goebbels.

Ch: I will advise Marshal Zhukov.

K: My first question: will the guns fall silent during the negotiations?

Ch: (Takes up the telephone receiver) Connect me with Marshal Zhukov. Report from Chuikov. General of Infantry Krebs is here. He is authorised by the German government to negotiate with us. He confirms that Hitler has committed suicide. I request that Party member Stalin be informed that Goebbels, Bormann and Grossadmiral Dönitz (according to Hitler's testament) have assumed power. Krebs is empowered to negotiate with us for an armistice. Krebs suggests a ceasefire during the negotiations. I will ask him now. (To Krebs) When did Hitler end his life?

K: Today at 15 hours 50. Pardon me, yesterday.

Ch: (Repeats) Yesterday at 15 hours 50. About peace? No, he has not spoken about that yet. I will ask him at once. Yes, understood, as ordered! (To Krebs) Marshal Zhukov asks if we are talking about a capitulation?

K: No, there are other possibilities.

Ch: He says there are other possibilities of making peace. No. This other government has turned to the Allies and is looking for other ways. If Krebs knows that? He has not mentioned it yet. (Krebs listens tensely.) They have no contact with the Allies. Krebs is only empowered to negotiate with the USSR. (Chuikov listens to the Marshal's instructions.) Yes . . . yes . . . he is empowered by Goebbels, the Reich Chancellor, and Bormann remains the Party leader. He says we are the first they have told about Hitler's death and his Testament. You, Party member Marshal, and I. (Pause) You want to ask Moscow? I will wait by the receiver. Understood. Krebs is not empowered, but he can talk about it. Good . . . Understood, Party member Marshal! I shall ask. And with the others? Understood, I have understood. (To Krebs) We can only negotiate with you for a total capitulation to the USSR and also to the USA and Britain.

K: In order to have an opportunity to discuss your demand I request a temporary ceasefire. (Conversation between Chuikov and Krebs)

Ch: (into the telephone) He cannot negotiate a total capitulation while he does not know the overall situation with the new government of Germany . . . he is only empowered to negotiate. Yes. I will ask him. (To Krebs) Do you wish to capitulate immediately?

K: I would have to discuss that with my government. It may be that a new government will be set up in the south. Until now there is only the government in Berlin. We request an armistice.

Ch: (into the telephone) They are requesting an armistice for negotiations. It may be that there will be a joint government in Germany. (Zhukov's voice is heard in the receiver) Yes, understood, good . . . I hear you, I understand. How? Good, as ordered! (To Krebs) The question of an armistice can only be decided on the basis of a total capitulation.

K: Then you will take over the area in which the government has residence and kill all the Germans.

Ch: We have not come to annihilate the German people.

K: (attempts to argue) The Germans will have no chance to work . . .

Ch: The Germans are already working with us.

K: (repeats) We request that you recognise the German government until the full capitulation, place yourself in contact with it and give us the chance to have contact to your government . . .

Ch: We have a condition – total capitulation.

K: But we believe the USSR will consider a new, legal German government. That is advantageous and favourable for both sides.

(0440 hours. The general makes a fresh request for a temporary armistice.)

K: Just a temporary . . . (K speaks in Russian). I cannot enter into other negotiations. It is in your interest to undertake these with the new German government. Gentlemen, I am only a plenipotentiary. I cannot answer in place of my government.

Ch: My offer is unequivocal.

K: The German government is hypnotising you? . . . You are the strong party, that we know and you believe it too.

Ch: Naturally we know that, and you must know it. You will keep fighting in vain and lose people. I ask you, what is the point in your fighting on?

K: We shall fight to the last man.

Ch: I am waiting for the total capitulation.

K: No! (The Soviet generals, Krebs, the young German officer and the interpreter in the room are silent. There is a large map of Berlin on the table.)

Ch: I, as a military man, am only interested in one thing – to defeat the enemy on the battlefield. We demand total capitulation.

K: If the Berlin garrison is destroyed there will be no legal German government.

Ch: Rubbish.

K: I have acquainted you with my role. I have no other.

Ch: I have informed you of the single and final condition: unconditional surrender. (The telephone rings again.) They have no possibility of communicating. They want to keep Hitler's death and Will a secret so that Himmler will not use it. Apparently they are also afraid of Dönitz. They want to announce it with our cooperation after an armistice. Himmler talked with them and was expelled from the Party . . . Very well! (To Krebs) The best solution for everybody who wants the new government to be recognised is capitulation.

K: Unconditional?

Ch: Unconditional.

K: (stubbornly) I am not authorised to negotiate the capitulation. If I did I would pre-empt the government. (He speaks occasionally in German, occasionally in Russian.)

Ch: But bullets do not distinguish between who is a soldier and who a member of the government.

K: (in Russian) I am uneasy thinking about this peace agreement.

Ch: We insist on the general demand made by ourselves and our allies – unconditional surrender.

(Chuikov informs himself by telephone about the situation on the ground. Army general Sokolovski enters. He is informed of Hitler's suicide, the Will, about Dönitz and Bormann etc. '10 hours 15.' The telephone rings. The Soviet government gives its final answer, a general capitulation or at least the surrender of Berlin. If this is rejected artillery bombardment of the city resumes at 10 hours 15.)

Lieut-Gen. Duchanov: I will give the order.

K: I do not have unlimited authority. We shall have to resume fighting and all will end horrendously. The surrender of Berlin is equally impossible. Goebbels cannot authorise it without Dönitz's agreement. (The telephone rings. It is reported that the colonel sent by the general could not cross the frontlines and was killed in a skirmish.)

K: That is a great misfortune. Can I talk with the interpreter? I had asked for a temporary ceasefire.

Ch: We are not shooting, the Germans are shooting.

Sokolovski: We will not discuss an armistice or separate negotiations.[1]

Goebbels told me that Krebs was to attempt to obtain agreement for the new German government to withdraw freely from Berlin. This was strongly urged particularly by Bormann. He was hoping this would be possible and had started preparing. Personally I did not think they would allow it; Hitler's assessment of the Russians had encouraged no such possibility. Thus we awaited the return of Krebs and passed the time making plans and searching for a clue as to how things would proceed without the Führer. I surprised myself with thoughts that had not been possible previously. Probably others did too. While we were convinced as long as Hitler lived that we would die with him voluntarily if it came to it, now we no longer thought in that way. Suddenly we seemed to have been released. With Hitler's death everything died, fell away, everything that had constituted our lives for years. We saw ourselves on the threshold of a future even before the past had opened the door to it, for everywhere the bitter fighting went on, and soldiers, old men, women and children still died.

After Krebs returned to the Reich Chancellery from the Russians at 1400 hours and reported that Bormann's hopes were illusory, there

---

1 Lew Besymenski, *Die Letzten Notizen von Martin Bormann: Ein Dokument und Sein Verfasser*, Stuttgart 1974, pp.276ff.

occurred a 'trial of strength' that would have been impossible during Hitler's lifetime. Bormann accused Krebs of not presenting his requirements to the Russians with sufficient skill. He even boasted that he could get a better result than Krebs had obtained simply by telephoning. Since the telephone lines were all down, he could not prove his point. Thus, as if Hitler were still alive, he demanded that the 'Citadel commandant', SS-Brigadeführer Mohnke, restore them at once, which Mohnke was not prepared to do, the reason being, as he told Bormann with great self-confidence, was that he was not going to send his men to their deaths unnecessarily. At last Bormann seemed to understand that without Hitler he was nothing.

For Dr Joseph Goebbels, the new Reich Chancellor, it was not apparent until now that he and his wife Magda would commit suicide in Berlin this same day. After the experiences of recent days and weeks hardly anything could shock us men any more, but the women, the female secretaries and chambermaids were 'programmed' differently. They were fearful that the six beautiful Goebbels children would be killed beforehand. The parents had decided upon this course of action. Hitler's physician Dr Stumpfegger was to see to it. The imploring pleas of the women and some of the staff, who suggested to Frau Goebbels that they would bring the children – Helga, Holde, Hilde, Heide, Hedda and Helmut – out of the bunker and care for them, went unheard. I was thinking about my own wife and children who were in relative safety when Frau Goebbels came at 1800 hours and asked me in a dry, emotional voice to go up with her to the former Führer-bunker where a room had been set up for her children. Once there she sank down in an armchair. She did not enter the children's room, but waited nervously until the door opened and Dr Stumpfegger came out. Their eyes met, Magda Goebbels stood up, silent and trembling. When the SS doctor nodded emotionally without speaking, she collapsed. It was done. The children lay dead in their beds, poisoned with cyanide. Two men of the SS bodyguard standing near the entrance led Frau Goebbels to her room in the

Führer-bunker. Two and a half hours later both she and her husband were dead. The last act had begun.

Chapter 18

I Flee the Reich Chancellery:
Russian Captivity

THE PREPARATIONS NOW BEGAN for the break-out by night from the Citadel, the rather obvious cover-name for the New Reich Chancellery. Bormann told Mohnke that, as the most senior in rank, he (Bormann) should take command. The SS general, who did not think much of Bormann and had been extremely firm with him over the telephone cable affair accepted the claim but made arrangements first for generals Krebs and Burgdorf to shoot themselves, which they did after downing a few bottles of alcohol for Dutch courage.

In ten mixed groups consisting of soldiers, women and other civilians, we were to attempt to flee the Citadel and head for the Berlin city boundary in a northerly direction (and using as far as possible the underground railway tunnels). Mohnke suggested to Bormann that they should set out together, but the Reichsleiter, now 'Party minister' clearly lacked the spirit for it. He sent his secretary Else Krüger with the Mohnke group and decided: 'I am going with the third troop to which Stumpfegger, Baur and Naumann are attached.' Thus he wanted to break through the Russian lines with Hitler's doctor, his flight captain and state secretary Werner Naumann, who had military experience and was listed as troop leader. In his decision to go with Naumann, Bormann was probably taking into account that Naumann had been appointed Propaganda

Minister in the new Reich cabinet in Hitler's Will. In a future meeting with Reich president Dönitz, whom Bormann despised, Naumann could therefore be very useful for Bormann.

I teamed up with SS-Obersturmbannführer Erich Kempka. In full uniform we climbed through a window of the New Reich Chancellery cellar. Under a hail of shell and mortar fire we crossed Friedrich-Strasse to the railway station where a couple of our panzers were standing and still offering the Russians battle. Towards midnight on the Weidendamm bridge we came upon Stumpfegger, Baur and Bormann who had lost their bearings, arrived by a roundabout route and were now separated from the Russians by an anti-tank barrier. As three of our panzers and three armoured vehicles rolled up, Bormann decided to break through the Russian lines using a panzer. Kempka jumped up, stopped the vehicles and told the leading panzer commander what was required. Under the protection of this panzer heading for the tank barrier, Bormann, Naumann and Stumpfegger doubled forward while I watched. The panzer was hit by a projectile from a Panzerfaust. The people alongside it were tossed into the air like dolls by the explosion. I could no longer see Stumpfegger nor Bormann. I presumed they were dead, as I told the Russians repeatedly in numerous interrogations later.

Now fifteen to twenty strong, once we realised we could not save our skins in this manner, we decided to go through the tramway tunnel. We reached See-Strasse, but only with great effort, losing people on the way. For a moment or so I had been alone with a member of the SS bodyguard when I heard the sound of tanks and voices through a shaft leading up to the street. I stopped and listened. From above I heard the call: 'German panzers are advancing. Come up, comrades!' I leaned out of the shaft and saw a German soldier, He looked towards me and beckoned. Scarcely had I left our hiding place than I saw all the Soviet tanks around me. The German soldier belonged to the Nationalkomitee Freies Deutschland formed after the Battle of Stalingrad to work for the communists. I was captured, but that was all. Although in full 'war paint' and not resembling a war-worn soldier, nobody was interested in me. German civilians passed by and talked to us, so far as was possible under the circumstances. I smuggled a gold watch which Hitler had given me with a personal inscription to a woman who spoke to me. She promised that since she had my name, which was also engraved on the watch, she would return it as soon as it was all over. An illusion. I never saw her again. A Russian sergeant approached me and said: 'Nichts gut, kamarad, uniform carry bird on arm. Nichts gut. Take off.' I understood: the silver eagle and swastika on the left upper sleeve of my uniform indicated that I was SS. I took his advice and ripped off the rank insignia and the offending 'bird on my arm', and tossed them away. The Führer always portrayed the Russians as bad, I thought, but they do not seem to be. On the contrary they offered me cigarettes and tobacco and even let me retain my two pistols, something that I found remarkable, since I was carrying one openly in my SS belt.

Under guard we walked for some days until we reached Posen. On the way we rested up once in an open field and on another occasion in a ruined church, and were treated as 'a classless society'. Everybody was equal to everybody else. Nobody enjoyed any advantage, nobody any unnecessary or unjustified disadvantage. That changed at Posen. Without warning I was locked in a potato cellar. The Russians had noticed the good-quality uniform I wore, as they told me later. In their opinion I must be somebody from Hitler's immediate staff. I was interrogated and had to write out who I was, my rank and what military posts I had had, and where I had served. I put down that I had been with an army unit in charge of catering. My real identity and what I had actually been doing since 1933 I kept secret, but it did not help me much, for one day I was brought back for interrogation and confronted with my past. Hans Baur, who had been in the military hospital and had stated truthfully that although a Luftwaffe general he had been Hitler's personal pilot, which the Russians refused to believe, had named me as a witness, and said I was in the camp. My disguise was blown. I had to write down the answers to all their questions which I had answered falsely before, but this time honestly.

The result was that one day two Russian officers appeared and escorted me by train to Moscow where I was thrown into the notorious Lubljanka Prison. There in a filthy bug-infested cell I waited, expecting the worst. It came in the form of a large GPU lieutenant-colonel who spoke good, cultivated German. He interrogated me with a monotonous patience which brought me to a state of sheer despair. Over and over he asked the same questions, trying to extract from me an admission that Hitler had survived. My unemotional assertion that I had carried Hitler's corpse from his room, had poured petrol over it and set it alight in front of the bunker was considered a cover story. In order to lull me into a false sense of security, he occasionally told me that before the war he had been in Germany, and he chatted with me as though he were an old war comrade. I remained as alert as I could, no easy task for the bed-bugs gave me no respite and only rarely did I sleep. Finally the bugs were even too much for the officer who had to watch me constantly. 'Tell the commissar', he advised me. When I replied with a cynical grin that if I did that they would increase the bug population, he countered: 'Tell him!' I did so, and could scarcely believe the result. I was moved to a 'lavish cell' with parquet flooring. Slowly it dawned on me why. It had been expected that I would complain.

Now came the carrot-and-stick treatment. Since I would not confirm what the commissar wanted to hear I had to strip naked and bend over a trestle after being warned that I would be thrashed if I did not finally 'cough up'. Naked and humiliated I persisted with my account: 'Adolf Hitler shot himself on 30 April 1945. I burned his body!' The commissar ordered a powerfully built lieutenant holding a whip with several thongs: 'Give it to him.' As I cried out like a stuck pig, he observed cynically: 'You ought to know about this treatment better than us. We learned it from your SS and Gestapo.'

Nevertheless I kept to the facts. He changed the procedure only inasmuch as he had me brought to a sound-proofed room – dressed again – where seven or eight commissars were waiting. The ceremony began once more. While somebody roared monotonously: 'Hitler is alive, Hitler is alive, tell the truth!' I was whipped until I bled. Near madness I yelled until my voice failed. Still bellowing the torturers in officers' uniform stopped for a rest. I was allowed to dress and returned to my cell where I collapsed. That was the beginning of an intensive interrogation strategy which even today gives me nightmares.

About a year after the end of the war I was thrust into a barred railway wagon and transported like some wild animal back to Berlin. My daily rations were a salted herring, 450 grams of damp bread and two cubes of sugar. In Berlin I was put into a jail. What the Russians wanted was to be shown was where – according to me – Hitler had shot himself. I was taken to the ruins of the New Reich Chancellery where a number of commissars and Marshal Sokolovski awaited. I showed them the sofa on which Hitler had shot himself, still where we had left it, but meanwhile ripped by 'souvenir hunters'. After this local visit, for which the Russians seemed to have little enthusiasm, I was returned to the prison for more interrogations.

These Berlin interrogations were carried out in a different way to those in Moscow. A female interpreter asked politely, I responded in like manner. The only thing certain was that the Russians did not believe me. In 1950 they were still doubtful that Hitler was dead. Accordingly the question-and-answer game in Berlin went round in monotonous circles. 'How much blood sprayed on the carpet?' 'How far from Hitler's foot did the pool of blood extend?' 'Where was his pistol exactly?' 'Which pistol did he use?' and 'How and where was he sitting exactly?' These were some of the stereotype, endlessly repeated questions I was obliged to answer. The interpreter was hearing these details for the first time and they interested her, but even so it was not hard to see that she would have preferred to be doing something else. The questioning usually went on without interruption until the bread trolley was heard.

One day when I had had just about enough of the same stupid questions I reacted stubbornly as the trolley passed. 'That is the end of it', I said, 'I am hungry and cannot go on.' The interpreter reacted with a friendly smile and the observation that she was from Leningrad and knew 'what hunger really was'. 'When you tried to starve us out', she went on with a blush, 'we ate mice and rats.' I was ashamed of my outburst and fell silent. The interrogation ended.

Measured by the term of my imprisonment, Berlin was only a flying visit. Soon I was back in the Moscow prison where, a long time later, I met Otto Günsche again. In the prison hospital we were treated with kid gloves in order to show us how good things could get. One day it was revealed to us that we were to have the opportunity to write our 'memoirs'. We were released from hospital and given rooms in a Moscow villa in which the widow of a general lived. After she had got to know and trust us, she told me that her son had often been seen in public with Stalin. Under guard we now set down on paper, day in, day out, our experience of Hitler. Then before we had really got used to the house and surroundings, it was time to move on. We arrived at a villa outside Moscow. German soldiers served us as they had General Seidlitz, captured at Stalingrad, and who had been our predecessor in this dacha. It was not a bad life. The food was good and we were decently treated. Suddenly it was not so important to the Russians where Hitler might have gone. They wanted manuscripts which proved that his main aim had been to play the Russians for fools – if necessary with the Western Powers. According to the Soviets we knew more about this than was in the official documents.

Our career as historians came to an end when the Russians realised that we were not prepared to portray Molotov's negotiations with Hitler falsely. Without blinking an eye they denied that for a period Stalin and Hitler had made common cause and shared out

Poland between them. Our 'memoirs' were archived. We became normal PoWs and were put into a camp for generals. It contained forty-two generals and three staff officers. Although we lived well there, the other inhabitants made us sick. Looking at these idlers, pedlars swapping little boxes and other nonsense, I asked myself how the 'Boss' could have expected to win the war with them. Most of the gentlemen complained about the rations prescribed by the Russians for the other ranks service personnel, comprised of German PoWs, demanding that cigarettes and sugar be excluded. As Günsche and I were on the side of the men in this quarrel, eventually the generals refused to return our salutes. Although there were exceptions, they could not wash away the negative impression. The generals went home to Germany. We, the two 'Hitler people', were put on trial in 1950 and received twenty-five years' hard labour in the Soviet Union.

When Red Army soldiers fetched us from the now empty camp and brought us to the prison where we were to be tried, I thought I would never see Germany again. At first we asked ourselves if it was to be a military or civilian trial. In vain. There was no clue. The judges wore robes, and there were uniformed officers sitting around, but this told us nothing, for men in officers' uniform also worked part-time in factories, as carpenters and at work benches. Scarcely had I become accustomed to the dim courtroom, which reminded me of a school hall with its red curtains, than I heard the charges against me from the lips of the interpreter. I had 'helped Hitler to power', had known his 'criminal plans' and supported him 'with conspiratorial intent'. My speechlessness at these charges was apparently accepted as a guilty plea. Within ten minutes the pompous theatre was ended. Each of us got twenty-five years. A Russian tried to console me. He gave me a friendly slap on the shoulder and said: 'Comrade, twenty-five years is not so much. It could have been more. You will soon be home.' I did not believe him.

Five years later, I was in a railway coach on my way to West Germany. I had served Hitler to the end, and in the opinion of the Russians by 1955 I had paid the price.

Index